Healing in the Hebrew Months

Prophetic Strategies Hidden in the Tribes, Constellations, Gates, and Gems

Seneca Schurbon

Copyright © 2019 Seneca Schurbon

All rights reserved. This book is protected by the copyright laws of the United States of America. No portion of this book may be stored electronically, transmitted, copied, reproduced, or reprinted for commercial gain or profit without prior written permission from Seneca Schurbon. Permission requests may be emailed to seneca@freedom-flowers.com. Only the use of short quotations for reviews or as reference material in other works is allowed without written permission.

All Scripture quotations, unless otherwise indicated, are taken from the New International Version®, NIV®. Copyright ©1973, 1978, 1984, 2011 by Biblica, Inc.TM Used by permission of Zondervan. All rights reserved worldwide. www.zondervan.com The "NIV" and "New International Version" are trademarks registered in the United States Patent and Trademark Office by Biblica, Inc.TM

Scripture taken from the New American Standard Bible® (NASB), Copyright © 1960, 1962, 1963, 1968, 1971, 1972, 1973, 1975, 1977, 1995 by The Lockman Foundation. Used by permission. www.Lockman.org

Scripture taken from the New King James Version®. Copyright © 1982 by Thomas Nelson. Used by permission. All rights reserved.

Scripture quotations marked KJV are taken from the 1769 King James Version of the Holy Bible, Public Domain.

Scripture quotations marked ESV are taken from The Holy Bible, English Standard Version® (ESV®) copyright © 2001 by Crossway Bibles, a publishing ministry of Good News Publishers. Used by permission. All rights reserved.

Available from Amazon.com, freedom-flowers.com, and other retail outlets where applicable.

ISBN: 978-1-7333795-0-2

Disclaimer

I am not a doctor, licensed dietitian or licensed counselor. The information in this book should not be seen as medical, nutritional, or mental health advice and is not intended to take the place of consulting licensed health care professionals. Check with your doctor, dietitian, counselor, and/or other health professional before implementing any of the suggestions outlined in this book.

Table of Contents

Introduction	1
The Hebrew Calendar	3
The Twelve Tribes	7
The Constellations	13
The Gemstones	25
The Gates of Jerusalem	31
The Flower Essences	35
Rosh Chodesh	37
Stepping Outside Time	41
Times and Seasons Chart	45
Nisan ניסן	47
Iyar אייר	59
Sivan סיון	71
Tammuz תמוז	79
Av אב	89
Elul אלול	99
Tishrei תשרי	107
Cheshvan חשון	115
Kislev כסלו	123
Tevet טבת	131
Shevat שבט	139
Adar אדר	147
Your Birth Month	155
Onward	161
References	165

Introduction

Several years ago, I had a dream. A voice was telling me that every weed has a season in which it's vulnerable and can be effectively dealt with. The voice said not to waste time and effort on the wrong weeds for the season. I thought that was interesting and seemed wise, but I wasn't sure how to recognize which season was for what weed or how to apply what I learned in practical terms. I promptly forgot about the dream and walked right into learning about the meanings behind the Jewish months. A friend mailed me some info on the month we were in, and I began to see the possibilities for tapping into each season on a deeper level. I developed a program in a matter of weeks and have been refining it over the last few years. Later, I looked back at my dream journal and realized that I had been walking out my dream.

Introduction

When we follow the schedule God laid out in the stars, freedom in certain areas comes more easily as we take advantage of specific blessings. God wants to bring forth specific things in our lives every month that will propel us forward into our destiny.

Each of the following come together to give us strategy throughout the year: the explanations behind each Hebrew month, the original meaning of the corresponding constellations, the tribes that correlate to each, and the gates of Jerusalem. When we align all these together, blessings, areas of healing, potential pitfalls, and warfare are revealed.

We begin in the month of Nisan, which starts in March or April. The first few months follow the story of the exodus and the journey to the promised land. It's a time of breaking out of bondage and moving into all God has for us. We can repeat this cycle year after year because we always have areas of our lives where we are not living in our full potential. In some cases, we miss a crucial step and have to go round the mountain again; in other cases, it simply wasn't time for the exact freedom we had in mind, but we became untangled in other areas. We also get ourselves into new situations and then have to get out. Every Nisan is a fresh start, but you can join during any month of the year.

The Hebrew Calendar

It's a bit of a challenge to follow the Hebrew calendar for those of us who are accustomed to the standard Gregorian calendar. The Hebrew months seem to start all over the place when compared with the Gregorian months. Holidays seem to move, and occasionally, the Hebrew calendar has a thirteen-month year. The Hebrew calendar employs three different astronomical occurrences: the rotation of the earth around the sun, the rotation of the earth on its axis, and the rotation of the moon around the earth. Our Gregorian calendar doesn't follow any of these, and dates are set arbitrarily.

Each month begins on a new moon, the first visible crescent in the sky. A Jewish day begins at sundown before what we would consider a day, so if a new moon begins on the fourth of a Gregorian month, the day would actually start at sundown on the third.

Lunar calendars drift slightly over time. If each month is twenty-nine or thirty days, then the year is eleven days shorter than it should be. That doesn't seem like a problem until you have too many short years back-to-back, and then the feast days are out of whack with harvest times (important in ancient times), and the whole schedule goes way off track.

In ancient times, the Sanhedrin noticed this by looking at the development of the crops, livestock, and weather, and if it didn't look like spring, they had an additional Adar. Now it's corrected by having an extra Adar every two or three years. Hebrew leap years follow a Metonic cycle, which means that leap years occur seven times within a nineteen-year period. Years 3, 6, 8, 11, 14, 17, and 19 have an additional Adar.

The bigger picture is why we would want to follow these seasons. The cyclical patterns of time carry imprints of the past for good or bad. If you've ever noticed that a certain time of year is always difficult for you, you've experienced this. But the victories, the feasts, the times that we know God is going to meet with us on a certain topic—those we milk for all they're worth. The more we take advantage of those patterns, the stronger and more significant they become. On specific negative dates in Jewish history, such as the 9th of Av, many bad things have happened. We pull in the opposite direction of those so that we don't add strength and agreement to those outcomes.

While we recognize the cyclical patterns, time is linear too. We are always progressing toward a culmination in these areas. Cyclical meets linear to form a spiral staircase of our development, both corporately and individually. By applying these strategies, you can become more intentional about maximizing the positive patterns and breaking the negative ones.

To connect the two calendars, you can purchase printed Jewish calendars with the Gregorian dates on them. You can add a calendar app on your phone, and at the time of writing, iPhone has the Jewish calendar built in. You just need to turn it on in your calendar settings. HealingintheHebrewMonths.com has a free printable calendar with email reminders of when each month starts.

It also helps to have community with others following this different calendar system. Our Facebook group Healing in the "Hebrew Months Community" is one great place to find like-minded folks. Link to join can be found at HealingtheHebrewMonths.com

The Twelve Tribes

Traditionally, each of the twelve tribes of Israel have been associated with a specific month in the Jewish year. You might wonder why I associate different tribes with each month when other people use a different model. The people who are teaching that each month correlates with a tribe, Hebrew letter, sense, body part, and constellation are pulling their data from an ancient book, Sefer Yetzirah which they usually won't disclose because of the connections to Kabbalism. Sefer Yetzirah pre-dates Kabbalah; Kabbalah followers and occultists have picked up the concepts it contains and run with these, as it is a very mystical book. So have some messianic sources. Other people simply parrot the information without tracing it back to the source. I see bits of Masonic detail in the text as well, though it would predate freemasonry. Despite the book's questionable background, it might include valid information.

Sefer Yetzirah itself does not link any tribes to months within its texts, but in Kabbalah, each of the tribal patriarchs is a soul root from which the Jewish people descend. By extension, they placed the tribes correlating to the senses listed in Sefer Yetzirah, which happens to be marching order. I started with marching order, but didn't feel that the months lined up correctly. The more I learned, the more I saw connections between the tribe's prophecies, their flags, and the constellations. When I laid them out according to what I was seeing, the revelation on each month worked.

Truth should confirm itself when it's correct. We can check the order by lining up all the twelves numerically, starting in the month of Nisan: twelve tribes, twelve months, twelve constellations, twelve gemstones, and twelve gates. I looked for layered revelation where these confirmed each other, and I had a hard time tying up everything so that it was neat and tidy when I tried to use the commonly held marching order of the tribes. Some of the information about the twelve tribes can be sourced biblically or in Jewish history, which connects all these topics.

In every case except the tribes, I've been able to lay out the patterns in order with Nisan as the starting point, and it just works. If you wanted to go by the law of first mention, you would put the tribes in birth order, but that didn't work. Neither did blessing order or camp order. God is a God of order, yet the tribes were never in the same order twice.

Therefore, I opted instead to match them with constellations since it was obvious and screaming at me. If you look at each tribe's banner or blessing, you will see constellation clues. You cannot convince me that the Lion of the tribe of Judah isn't Leo! But marching order has Judah with Aries the ram/lamb.

Joseph's prophecy was "With bitterness archers attacked him; they shot at him with hostility. But his bow remained steady." (Gen 49:23-24) I placed him with Sagittarius, the archer. Some connections are more subtle, and you find them in the decans or sub-constellations, which I'll get into more later. Some I had to place by faith and found the confirmation later as I looked into the meanings of gates or months. "Dan will be a snake by the roadside, a viper along the path that bites the horse's heels so that its rider tumbles backward." (Gen 49:17) Scorpio contains Ophichus, who has a heel wound, and Sagittarius, next to Scorpio, is a half-man–half-horse, and the fall back can be seen when Sagittarius descends lower in the sky than Scorpio. I'm not comfortable ignoring these significant points just to put the tribes in the customary marching order.

A few others like me have determined alternate placements, and we don't agree entirely either, but I see their logic and applaud them for thinking outside the box rather than following blindly. I appreciate anybody willing to question "the way we've always done it" and chart their own course. I'm not dogmatic enough to say I'm correct on all counts, but I think I'm much closer than some of what's out there. I will say, that when all the sets of twelve come together, they present a cohesive picture with each building upon the other. When we have trouble sorting truth, we can always look for confirmation.

I'm not going to be emphatic about how right I am, because I've changed my alignments several times, and I am not done learning. However, there are enough consistent themes that I feel my information connects well.

If we put the tribes in the order that I have them now, correlating to constellations, and look up the meanings of their names, we have a relevant message for our journey.

Gad: A fortune for which a troublesome, invasive effort is made

Asher: The nouns אשר ('esher), אשר ('ashar), and אשר ('osher) mean happiness or blessedness. Nouns אשור (ashur) and אשר (ashur) mean a step, a walk, or a going.

Benjamin: Son of my right hand

Zebulon: Glorious dwelling place

Judah: Let him be praised

Naphtali: My wrestlings

Levi: To join or connect

Dan: Judge, judgment

Joseph: Increaser, to add increase or repeat

Simeon: Hearing or hearing with acceptance

Rueben: A combination of two words: The first part comes from the verb ראה (ra'a), meaning to see or understand. The second part of the name Reuben is the word בן (ben), meaning son, offspring.

Issachar: Recompense

Putting it together: There is a fortune for those who are willing to make a troublesome, invasive effort. There are happiness and blessings for those who make a decisive progression forward. The son of my right hand will guide you to a glorious dwelling place. Let him be praised. Wrestlings (mental) joined with careful judgment bring an increased ability to hear, see, and inherit the recompense for your trouble.

The Constellations

Each month has a corresponding constellation and tribe, as I stated in the last chapter. When I was beginning to study biblical dream interpretation, I was fascinated with Joseph's dream of the eleven stars bowing down to him and the resulting resentment of his brothers. They all knew it was about them. Nobody had to come along and unpack that symbolism. They already knew that the constellations represented them.

But really, why wouldn't that be the case? God showed Abraham that he would be the father of many nations by the stars, and he was Jacob's (later known as Israel) grandpa.

Not only did Satan not create the zodiac, but the zodiac actually tells the story of the gospel. A coming savior, born of a virgin, the battle and defeat of the enemy, the rulership of Christ, and the redemption of the church is all overhead. Frances Rolleston did the pioneering work on the stars back in the 1800s. Though she was a Christian, she did not believe she would get spiritual cooties from looking at what other cultures and belief systems were doing and their sources of information. Her book, simply titled *The Mazzaroth* (taken from Job 38:32), broke the ground for others to begin to understand the purpose of the constellations beyond just a fortune-telling tool. Other Christian books out there on the zodiac borrow heavily (or simply repackage) her research, which is now public domain.

Each of the twelve constellations has smaller constellations around them called decans. They rise helically every ten days or about three times each month. Helical rising is the phenomenon when a decan becomes visible on the eastern horizon at dawn. Each day after, it rises slightly earlier and moves further westward until it has set on the opposite horizon. The way that decans interact with the main constellations tells us a lot, and we don't have a complete story without them. Modern astrology ignores them, but for our purposes, they unpack the story of triumph over evil and God's supreme reign.

Most cultures practicing ancient astronomy understand that there are forty-eight constellations (twelve main ones plus the thirty-six decans). Ptolemy and the Persians had forty-eight; the Egyptians and Persians both agree that there are twelve main constellations and thirty-six lesser ones. Beyond that, the names and pictures stay mostly the same across cultures and time. Virgo is a virgin that becomes supernaturally pregnant and gives birth to a son in nearly every culture. All you and I have to do is look up in the sky, see all the seeming randomness, and know that these cultures didn't just invent systems with the same symbolism. These would have to have been in place before people fanned out all over the world.

The oldest surviving work we have on the zodiac is the Phaenomena by Greek poet Aratus from the early third century B.C., which Paul quotes in Acts 17:28. As far as other early astronomers, Frances Rolleston states,

> The Egyptians, on whose early monuments the signs are found, acknowledged that they derived their astronomy from the Chaldeans. The Chaldeans attributed their science to Oannes, supposed to be Noah. The Arabs and Brahmins, among whom astronomy was early cultivated, seem to have derived it from Abraham, through Ishmael and the children of Keturah. The Greeks supposed their imperfect knowledge of the subject came through the Egyptians and the Chaldeans. The Romans are thought to have received through the Etrurians the names of the signs still in use among European nations. The Etrurians are considered to have derived them, with their other arts and sciences, from Assyria. The early Greek poet Hesiod is said to have made use of Assyrian records. He

mentions some of the constellations by the names they now bear.

According to Enoch, in "the book of the courses of the heavenly luminaries," the angel Uriel showed him the "signs, seasons, years, and days." Enoch 1 75:3 He calls the constellations "portals" that open in their appointed season. According to Josephus, the Jewish historian, the children of Seth "were the inventors of that peculiar sort of wisdom, which is concerned with the heavenly bodies, and their order." Job, the oldest book in the Bible, estimated to date between 1900 and 1700 B.C., mentions a number of constellations by name.

Psalm 19 makes our clearest and most compelling case for the mazzaroth. My commentary is in parentheses below.

The heavens (the celestial arena) declare the glory of God;
And the firmament (expanse of heaven) shows His handiwork.
Day unto day utters speech,
And night unto night reveals knowledge.
There is no speech nor language
Where their voice is not heard.
(The zodiac defies all language and cultural barriers.)
Their line has gone out through all the earth,
(The line sounds a bit like the lines that make up a star chart, connecting each to form a picture like the dot-to-dot drawings we did as kids.)
And their words to the end of the world.

The Constellations

In them He has set a tabernacle for the sun,
(Tabernacle is a dwelling place, tent, or house. House is a common term in astronomy and astrology.)
Which is like a bridegroom coming out of his chamber,
(Jesus is the bridegroom; this is his story, start to finish.)
And rejoices (the joy that was set before him) like a strong man to run its race.
Its rising is from one end of heaven,
And its circuit to the other end;
And there is nothing hidden from its heat (Psalm 19:1–6 NKJV).

Without further ado, let's get into the star sequence. I'll try to be brief so that you aren't overwhelmed with the details, because to do this topic justice, you need a stand-alone book, and several are available on the market. I'll also include additional comments within each month.

We begin in Virgo. Many scholars think the Sphinx is a mnemonic device, which reminds us to start with the woman and end with the lion. Virgo is the virgin, holding a branch with four sections. In the Old Testament, Jesus is named the Branch of David (Jeremiah 23:5; 33:15), the Branch of My Servant (Zechariah 3:8), the Branch of Man (Zechariah 6:12), and the Branch of Jehovah (Isaiah 4:2).

In Libra, we have the scales. Two stars on each balance are opposite each other. This represents our inability to pay for our own damages and Christ's ability to cover for us. Decans of Libra are the Crux or cross; Lupus, the victim slain; and the Corona or crown.

Scorpio or the scorpion is being crushed by Ophiuchus, a decan of Scorpio, but Scorpio is also attacking Ophiuchus on the other heel. Ancient Egypt uses a snake rather than a scorpion, but we're to tread on both of those (Luke 10:19). This sign is reminiscent of the prophecy in Genesis 3:15 that God gave to Satan. "And I will put enmity between you and the woman, and between your offspring and hers; he will crush your head, and you will strike his heel." Meanwhile, in a nearby decan, Serpens is going after the Crown, and Ophiuchus is holding him down.

Sagittarius the archer is aiming directly at the heart of Scorpio and lifting his forefoot in a limp. (The head smashing and injured heel seem to be themes throughout this star story.) Lyra the harp represents the rejoicing in heaven. Ara the fiery altar is tipped over and heading downward as God's wrath is being poured out on Satan. The last decan is Draco the dragon, whose head is being stomped on by Hercules, who again, has a hurt foot.

Then we have Capricorn, the goat with a fishy tail. He is down and dying. The goat represents Christ's sacrifice. (Goats and lambs were sacrificial animals, which is where we got the term "scapegoat.") The fish represents his nature as a man. (Fish have typically been the sign of God's people.)

In Aquarius, we have a man pouring out water from a large urn into the mouth of a fish. Water often represents the Holy Spirit and baptism.

Pisces has two fishes tied together with a band, and they are swimming in different directions. People interpret this differently, but all agree that the fish represent people going in two different directions, typically, before and after Christ. It could also represent two different streams of believers within the church, or a believer's relationship with God and moving out into the world as evangelism. They are bound to Cetus the sea monster, but Aries is intervening.

Aries the ram falls in line with Passover but in our overall gospel story, this is not the dying lamb. This is the one who was slain before the foundation of the world (Revelation 13:8) and who is worthy to open the seals (Revelation 5). This is an overcomer, crushing the head of the sea monster and claiming the fish as his own.

Taurus the bull is coming out of Aries and raging toward his enemy. He has to step on Cetus the sea monster too.

Gemini the twins are less obvious; they are sitting peacefully unified, their weapons at the ready but not actively positioned. This is likely after their hard won battle. The harp in the hand of one might represent worship and rejoicing. This could represent Christ and the church as Scripture does tell us that when we see him, we'll be like him (1 John 3:2).

Cancer the crab is said to be the most changed from its original meaning. We don't have a Hebrew word for this constellation. When we consider star meanings, we can possibly deduce that it has something to do with a pastoral setting with cattle-folds, sheepfolds, and two donkeys. The main consensus is that it's a final resting place for the church. Because so many different cultures have this constellation as a crab, I prefer not to brush it aside and change it from an unclean creature into something we think fits more easily with our understanding. Peter had a vision of the unclean animals and recognized this meant the salvation of Gentiles too. The crab is a creature born of water as is the church with many legs. The translation of sheepfolds might apply as Jesus did say that he had other sheep not of this fold (John 10:16).

Last but certainly not least, we have Leo. Leo is obvious—the Lion of the tribe of Judah, ruling and reigning.

So where did our understanding of the constellations go wrong? I considered the watchers (fallen angels) when they came down, because they taught many things we weren't supposed to be getting into, including astrology. I thought of Daniel and the collision of his culture with an occultic system. Nimrod and the Tower of Babel have implications for the constellations too. Astrology has been corrupt for a very long time. Of course, the enemy couldn't let something as huge as a prophecy in the stars of his demise and our redemption that supersedes all cultural and language barriers get out.

If you dig into further study of the constellations on your own, I would advise you to keep your skeptic's hat on, even when it comes to Christian books on the mazzaroth. As I said earlier, most of these borrow heavily from Frances Rolleston. Her research is mostly excellent and tries for impartiality, but I'm not entirely sold on her translations of star names. Here is her explanation.

> The names are here explained on the supposition that the first language was given by the Creator to the first man, conveying ideas to the mind by sounds, as impressions of form and colour are conveyed by sight. In all languages these sounds are traceable, conveying the same idea. In the dialects of the most ancient and earliest civilized nations, they are the most recognizable; in those of the most barbarous, the most obscured. This primitive language appears to have been spoken by Noah from the names given by him to his sons. In the confusion of the lip at Babel, pronunciation, not words or roots, were altered. This may be inferred from the presence of Hebrew roots in the dialects of all nations.

What this means is that in the case of a foreign word that sounds like a Hebrew word, she used the

Hebrew meaning. As an example, the Arabic word *deneb* means "tail" in Arabic and is often a star in the actual tail of an animal in the constellation, but according to her system, it sounds like *diyn* which means "judge." I don't agree with overlooking the obvious to make a teaching fit my agenda.

I think we can sometimes use words that sound the same but not always. (If you think about it, you can see how confusing this is in English as well.) I don't think we can hang a revelation here, which is what I see people trying to do with Cancer. They are trying to untwist something they believe has been twisted, and in the process, they might be twisting it even further. Now Frances documents everything, so you can look at the name sources and make up your own mind. However, that is not what I see in other writings who parrot her without explaining that they derived that meaning from an Arabic word that sounds like a Hebrew word. They assume the same meaning that Frances used, and that is the case for all the topics mentioned in this book. These subjects are messy, and you're encouraged to exercise skepticism and use your noggin. Christians have to believe a lot of weird stuff in order to be Christians, and we operate heavily on confirmation bias. This is our undoing at times and why we can be sold on the word meaning "judge" because it conveniently fits the storyline and ignores that the literal translation is "tail." Most of our star names are Arabic, so either we do the tough research ourselves, or we do not hang any hats on star names. When I mention them in this book, I've found their meanings from a secular source without a Christian agenda.

I don't mind looking into the Greek mythology surrounding the constellations. Plato said that the Greeks adopted or translated the "barbarian names" and founded stories on the meaning in their own language. In some cases, I reverse engineer some of the Greek myths that actually sound like Bible stories.

Otherwise, I have nothing but mad respect for Frances, who took on a taboo subject during a time when women were only allowed to teach children. She spent fifty years of her life plumbing the depths of the teaching.

The Gemstones

Every one of the twelve tribes has a correlating stone. These stones were in the breastplate of the ephod that the high priest had to wear or else he couldn't come before God. According to the Talmud, the breastplate had to be worn to atone for the sins of the children of Israel. These twelve stones also correlate to the foundation of the New Jerusalem in Revelation 21:19. There is a lot of debate over which stone corresponds to which tribe, as well as how to translate the stones into their modern equivalents.

As an example of the confusion of the translation of the stone names, the fourth stone on the high priest's ephod is called "emerald" in the King James version (Exodus 28:18), "carbuncle" in the Greek translation (Septuagint), "turquoise" in the New American Standard version, and "garnet" in Strong's Concordance.

Almost everyone agrees on a few stones, which helps us get on the right track. *Odem* means "red stone," and the corresponding Greek was likely *sardios*. Almost everyone puts that together with *carnelian*.

The broad consensus is that *akhlameh* and *amethystos* are amethyst, which is no great surprise.

Sapir and *sappheiros* simply mean "blue stone." Historically, lapis was called sapphire, and sapphires, as we know them today, were not known at that time. They also are too hard to carve with rudimentary equipment. Most scholars agree that sapphire refers to lapis lazuli.

The experts are sure that *pitdah* and *topazion* are topaz. I'm not. My money is on olivine (peridot), which is the main claim to fame from the Egyptian island Topazios, now named Zabargad.

For our purposes, we are less concerned with exactly what the archaic names mean and will focus instead on what they symbolize.

Paul says in 1 Corinthians 3:12 that we are to build on the foundation, which is Jesus Christ, with gold, silver, and precious stones. Either we are building with those, or we are building with wood, hay, and stubble, and the fire will prove which we've used. He's talking about the temple, which is now you. You are the earthly habitation where God dwells in this era. How you build on your foundation of salvation determines how you will come through trials. This is not just nice little language; it contains instruction. Netanel Nickells of Righteous Foundations has a teaching on this called "Stones to Build on the Foundation of Yeshua," although he chooses different stones than I do.

Each stone symbolizes a tribe, and each tribe has redeeming characteristics as well as areas of weakness. For example, Simeon (with the gemstone of *chrysoprase*) struggles with anger and will have to deal with that. The foundation stones in New Jerusalem are compared to a bride, prepared and adorned for her husband (Revelation 21:2). We are now a kingdom of priests, and as we go before God with our stones or our issues that need purification, we become rock solid.

There have been numerous attempts to link tribes with gems. But Scripture does not tell us which tribe went with what gem. We can only speculate. We only have precise instructions about how to lay out the grid for the ephod with the stones. Josephus says that the shoulder pieces, which had six names on each side, were in birth order, but we do not know the order on the actual breastplate.

Some historians propose that the colors are most important and that representative stones were chosen for those colors. Numbers Midrash Rabbah (an ancient Jewish version of a Bible commentary) tells us that the stones matched the color of the background on each tribe's banner, so I've chosen to go with that. To further narrow down the choices, I'm going with stones that were soft enough for them to engrave at that time, large enough to hold a name, and popular with ancient Egyptians, which is where they got the stones (Exodus 12:35–36).

Another consideration is how the breastplate worked. The ephod was routinely necessary to get answers to questions from God. The Urim and Thummim, in particular, are mysteries, because for all the detail on creating the ephod, the temple, and everything in it, we have no additional information on these items. Apparently, we are not supposed to know more about them. Some have speculated that they are stones that give yes or no answers. Yet if we read all the accounts of consulting the ephod, the responses hold much more detail than a simple yes or no. The Mishnah Torah says that the stones on the breastplate actually lit up to give the answer. Since some stones glow naturally under the right circumstances, this idea might not be entirely far-fetched. According to geology.com, 15 percent of minerals have visible fluorescence. To add to that, some of the names have indicator meanings, such as "lightening" or "glowing coal." I downloaded a list of luminous stones, and as it happens, my prime suspects for the gems that fit all the other criteria are on it. However, according to Revelation 21:18, the spiritual light of God rendered even gold as transparent.

Additionally, I've looked at the healing properties of the stones to see if they might fit with the overall themes of the month and included a brief line or two about how the gems I've chosen relate to the monthly themes.

If you would rather rely solely on biblical sourcing as opposed to my mix of Midrash, practicality, and supposition, you can look at both John and Ezekiel's vision of the New Jerusalem, which has the twelve foundation stones that correlate to the twelve tribes. Ezekiel 48 tells us the order of the tribes on each side, and in Revelation 21, John lists the stones. But John viewed the city in an unusual order: east, north, south, and west, which gives me pause. I don't know that this perspective is reliable enough to match up the Greek stone name with the Hebrew version, hoping that John stated them in the order he initially described the walls. When you're in the spirit, you're also not necessarily viewing objects from ground level. I'm not ready to hang my hat on that and abandon Jewish oral tradition. If you want to be scriptural and try to follow what John outlines, remember to read right to left as they would have in Greek, so read the Bible in order. Start placing stones and tribes from the right corner of a side of the city and ending on the left corner as a person would view it.

In either case, because the correlation between the stones and tribes is unclear, they don't play a large part in this book. It's not necessary that we get them exactly right; we just need to understand that they symbolize a tribe, which has good and bad attributes. They were a symbol, borne on the priest's shoulders and over his heart before God. We are now New Testament priests and can still carry all these attributes forward in prayer, knowing that God is transformative and deals with all the impurities, making us his radiantly beautiful bride.

The Twelve Gates of Jerusalem

Jerusalem means "city of peace," and we know that's not true in the natural, but for NewJerusalem, the heavenly city, it sure fits. Our earthly Jerusalem has been the epicenter of turmoil, but the city is going through a process of overcoming and attaining the promises. That is as true for us as it is for the geographic capital of Israel. Some teachings use the twelve gates as a process for spiritual maturity. I don't disagree with them, but when we look at them as a monthly cyclical process rather than lifetime progression, we need to see things a bit differently.

After I had been tracking with the seasons for a while—matching tribes, months, gems, and constellations—I had another dream. I dreamt that people were trapped in the book of Nehemiah and I was helping them escape. While I believe that dream went far beyond this surface application, I added the twelve gates, which laid out nicely in the order listed in the Bible, and found that the repairers of each gate contain relevant messages for us.

While our primary focus is on becoming free, entering the promised land with the tribes, and following their journey, Nehemiah jumps ahead to promises fulfilled, yet Israel had let them slip away.

Sanballat the Horonite, Tobiah the Ammonite, and Geshem the Arab are the villains in the story, trying to interfere with Nehemiah's plans for rebuilding (Nehemiah 2.19; 4:1–3, 4:8, 4:11; 6:2, 6:6–8). The Horonites and Ammonites were two people groups God said to drive out of the promised land. Generations later, they were back, trying to undermine the rebuilding. This appears to be a picture of how we need to reinforce what our ancestors have conquered or take back ground that we have taken in the past in a previous seasonal cycle. (This means that you have not done something wrong if you need to keep fighting for freedom in a certain area. You are making progress. Keep going.)

As Nehemiah worked, the opposition came at him in the form of mockery, threats, and false reports (Nehemiah 2:19; 4:1–3, 4:8, 4:11; 6:2, 6:6–8). How many times have you begun to move toward a goal and heard the discouraging internal voice, "What makes you think you can even do that? Who do you think you are? You can't pull that off. Even if you manage, it won't work in the long run." Like Nehemiah and his men, sometimes we have to work with a trowel in one hand and a sword in the other, saying, "I cannot come down!"

The Flower Essences

Freedom Flowers, an essence company, is my primary business. As a little girl, I discovered the healing power of the frequencies of flower essences. These essences are natural remedies for emotional healing and spiritual development. Much different than essential oils, they don't have any scent and are typically used internally. Flower essences are safe to use with any other medications or supplements as they have no biochemical means of healing. Some flower essences and herbal supplements are derived from the same plants, but they serve two different purposes with different results. Each flower has its own specific therapeutic properties.

"Healing in the Hebrew Months" initially started as a monthly program within my flower essence business. When I saw the monthly themes, specific flowers that could help us in this journey began exploding in my head. I had already noticed trends in what people would order during certain times of the year. Many people seemed to be dealing with the same issues during the same months, and now it was finally starting to make sense.

I developed a subscription program called "Times and Seasons," where I looked at the upcoming month, made an essence blend for it and mailed it out in time to reach clients around the new moon. Gemstone jewelry is also included. God sprang the jewelry part on me at the last minute with a sweet message about stewarding gifts.

In the monthly chapters, I discuss relevant essences for each month. Many of my customers prefer to buy single essences rather than blends or the subscription, so I'm providing ideas that can be individually tailored to what you need. The descriptions here are very brief as they are not the focus of the book, and a more extensive description of each flower's healing properties can be found on my website, as can the subscription club details or the twelve bottles to take you through a year.

If flower essences are new to you, I have a free mini-course on my website that will tell you all about them. While they can be useful adjuncts, it is certainly not necessary to use them in your process through these months.

Rosh Chodesh

Rosh Chodesh is the first day of the new month. It actually begins on sundown the day before and continues until sunset the following day. Rosh Chodesh is Hebrew for "head of the month" and the new moon festival. Every month in ancient times, people watched for the new moon that began a new month. When two witnesses confirmed that they could see the new moon, the Sanhedrin leaders stood and declared, "The new month is sanctified." Then they would light a bonfire on the mountain.

There is no one particular way to celebrate Rosh Chodesh. While it's typically a joyous time, there are no laws about it, and even if there were, Jesus said, let no man judge you regarding the new moon celebration or Sabbath (Colossians 2:16).

Rosh Chodesh is significant for women. According to the story, they refused to give their jewelry to the men who were melting it down to build the golden calf to worship, (Exodus 32) so God gave them an extra holiday every month. (This is why the Times and Seasons subscription includes jewelry.) Some women take time off from housework at Rosh Chodesh. Guys, remember there is no male or female in Christ. (See Galatians 3:28).

According to tradition, God had them make the new calendar before leaving Egypt, because slavery involves following someone else's timeline with no control of your own. I like the idea of using Rosh Chodesh to remind me that I am under God's time.

Thus, for me, I acknowledge that it is Rosh Chodesh, pile on a bunch of jewelry, which impedes my working, and focus on the subject of time. I think about what I should be doing this month, if I am spinning my wheels and being ineffective with my time, and if the enemy is trying to change it.

Going forward, as you work through the year, you'll want to spend some time looking at your personal circumstances and at the information about each month and begin to engage with God about how it applies personally to you. This could be some Rosh Chodesh time. Remember those calendar resources I mentioned at the beginning? Those are a great way to keep track of when Rosh Chodesh falls every month.

It helps me to check in a couple of times mid-month and see if I am on this time table. It will also benefit you to journal about the correlations you are seeing in your life. This will help you understand even more in future cycles as you personally see events unfold.

I thought about building more structure into this with written prayers and more concrete action plans for each month. But you would undoubtedly miss much of the personal application for yourself. As you read, be tuned in to the little nuances that allow you to make this journey your own. Follow those with prayer. The information in this book is for engagement, not consumption.

Stepping Outside Time

The twelve tribes, each correlating to one of the constellations, camped facing the tabernacle in the four directions. A flag bearing a symbol of each of the four faces of the cherubim faced in each of the four directions: Man (Rueben), eagle (Dan), ox (Joseph), and lion (Judah). These also correlate with the four seasons and create a picture of time. As the earth orbits around the sun, the tribes encamp around the tabernacle or the Shekinah glory light of God.

But then Moses pitches a tent *outside* the camp. What's up with that? Despite this, God speaks to Moses face-to-face, as one speaks to a friend. It's commonly taught that they used this tent before the tabernacle was built and before Aaron and his sons were anointed. Once the tabernacle (fancy tent) was up and running, the other tabernacle (rudimentary tent) went away. On a surface reading and in some translations more than others, that appears to be so. But there are some issues with that thinking. In Exodus 40, the glory of the Lord filled the tabernacle, and Moses could no longer enter. Only the high priest could go in, and the Levites acted as bouncers, making sure no average Joes got in because they would die. But then in later texts, Moses is in the tabernacle again. Hebrew doesn't help with the explanation. Both references use the term *ohel moed*. Anybody could go in the rudimentary tent, and we know from Exodus 33:11 that Joshua was in there all the time. Exodus 33:7 says "whomever" could go in the tent. Miriam was there, too. She had leprosy and had to stay out for a week until she was clean. Ironically, I would imagine a week in God's presence would get rid of leprosy.

I theorize that whenever somebody other than a high priest was in the tabernacle, they were in this tent outside the camp. In Numbers 11, we have even more clarity that the rudimentary tent was still in use as a bunch of people left the "tabernacle" and re-entered the camp.

When I first started looking into this, I got bent out of shape because here's this guy, Moses, who helps set up the cycle that we follow until the end of days, and he's putting everything into position; laying out the rules, regs, and protocols; and making sure all the feasts are observed correctly. Yet he's also thumbing his nose at the system and having these impromptu sessions with God. So what was I doing with this Times and Seasons subscription box? Was I steering people wrong? Is outside the camp really where it's at? God is outside time, and maybe that's where we really find him, not just his glory.

But I wasn't looking carefully enough.

Moses didn't spend all his time outside in the rudimentary tent. He was very much involved in the camp. On the other hand, I have some questions about Joshua. It's not like we have to decide whether we are going to be innies or outies. We can flow back and forth as needed.

Additionally, it's pretty clear that God was inhabiting the tabernacle (fancy tent) all the time except when he moved out by cloud or pillar of fire so the Israelites could break camp and move on. Moses's tabernacle (rudimentary tent) was a place to meet with God. Moses gets the seventy elders and takes them to the tent, and God shows up (Numbers 11:24–25). Moses, Aaron, and Miriam go out, and God descends in a cloud (Numbers 12:4–5). Moses takes Joshua out there; God comes to speak (Deuteronomy 31:14–15). It's good enough to visit, but he doesn't want to live there.

For our purposes and application, we can follow the seasons as much as it helps us to do so. Whenever you have a need or a concern, step outside the season and talk to God about it. If you need it now, trust that he'll meet you there. You have options.

As a believer, you are a priest, a dispenser of the blood; you're a walking, talking tabernacle (the fancy kind), and you can go where you want to go.

The times and seasons were made to serve you; you are not to serve them. Don't get all religious and rigid about this information or its application. Be flexible and allow the Lord to lead you.

Times and Seasons

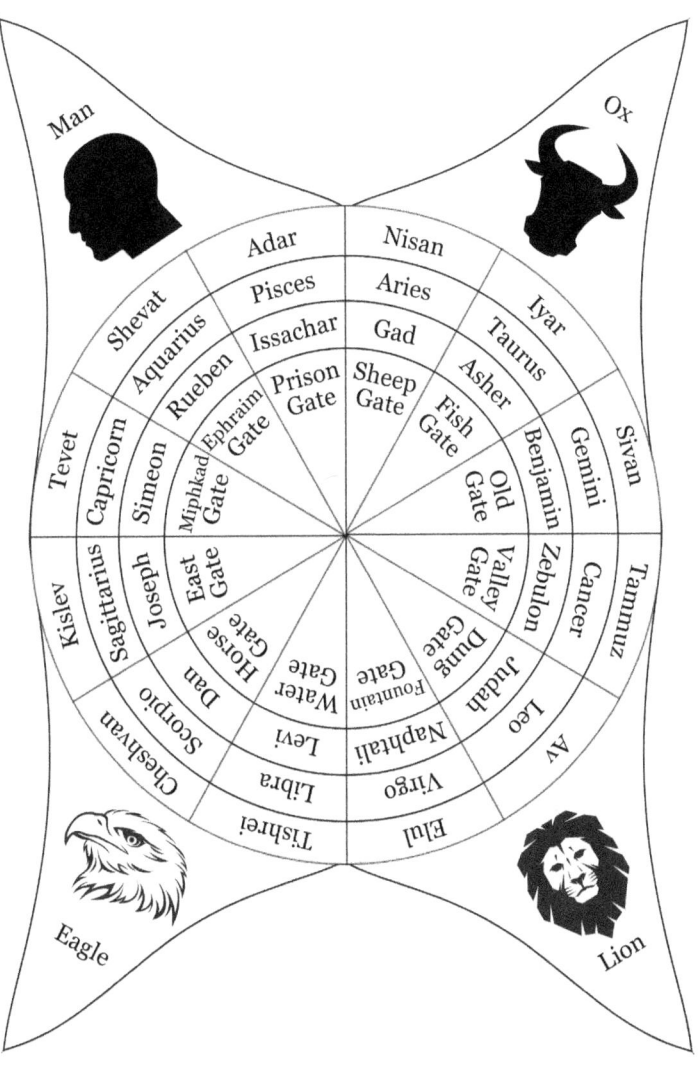

Healing in the Hebrew Months

Month at a Glance
Nisan ניסן

Starts in March or April

Meaning: To move or to start, miracles

Blessing: Redemption and freedom

Area of Healing: Enslavement

Action Needed: Declare yourself free from _____, and move or start toward your promised land

Warfare: Declare blessings over your negative situation

Holiday: Passover

Tribe: Gad

Gem: Gray agate

Gate: Sheep

Constellation: Aries the ram

Decans: Cassiopeia the enthroned woman, Cetus the sea monster, Perseus the breaker

Nisan ניסן

We spend some time being extra intentional during Nisan, because it's the beginning of our cycle. Nisan is when the exodus started. The first months of the Hebrew year follow the Israelites' journey to the promised land, and this cycle repeats with us. We move out of bondage in some areas and have the opportunity to step into what's been promised to us.

Depending on who you ask, Nisan either means "miracles" or "to move" or "to start." Personally, I'm claiming all these meanings, because I can see all those attributes in the history of the month.

Nisan is also referred to as "the month of redemption." According to the opinion of sages, "in Nisan, our forefathers were redeemed from Egypt, and in Nisan, we will be redeemed." During Nisan, God pulled his people out of Egyptian slavery and began the attempt to get them into the promised land. This is pivotal.

The wilderness is not about enduring a hard time in a bleak place. It's about stripping away false systems, cultured norms, and getting to know God in all his many facets. It forges in you the ability to take and steward your personal promised land. God has a process of getting us where we need to be, which does not need to take forty years. However, if we need to go around the mountain again, we always have that option. Over the next few months, we are leaning hard into that process, taking hold of the blessings, and avoiding the pitfalls.

This is the time to declare yourself free in whatever areas have enslaved you, and *to move* or *to start* toward your own promised land. Nisan is also associated with our speech. Just as God created the world with speech, we create with speech as well or at least our experience of it. A slave has no voice and thus has no power to shape their world using their free speech. We can only experience freedom when we declare ourselves free.

This works the other way as well. When we speak out of negativity, pessimism, and oppression, Jewish tradition says that we will have trouble for the rest of the year. To fully engage the power of Nisan, start speaking positively over your circumstances. Calendula flower essence helps us become conscious of how we are using our words and of the creative power behind them.

Nisan ניסן

The tribe associated with Nisan is Gad, which means "good fortune," according to the short version. During this month, we can take stock of the blessings that have happened over the previous year. We can increase in the coming year by walking in gratitude or by counting our blessings. Gad was also a war-like tribe, backing up Aries' secular reputation as warriors. "A troop shall overcome him, but he shall overcome at the last," said Jacob about Gad (Genesis 49:19 KJV). Our mindset needs to be that we will win in the end, no matter what it looks like right now. Our warfare needs to include strong and powerful declarations.

The longer meaning of Gad's name is, "a fortune for which a troublesome, invasive effort is made." Gad ended up with the best part of the promised land because they obeyed God and made the effort to fight for it. They, along with Rueben and Manasseh, fought for the land east of the Jordan but did not stop there when they had their own land. "We will not return to our homes until every Israelite has received his inheritance" (Numbers 32:18 ESV). They wanted nothing less than everything God had in mind for them and their newly freed nation.

Gad's flag was said to be a "mixture of black and white." We don't know if this simply meant gray or if it was truly black and white as we know it. I've chosen gray-banded agate for the tribal stone. Agate is purported to encourage you to explore unknown territory by instilling a sense of safety and security.

The star sign is Aries the ram. Aries does connect with Passover, and some have said the ram is really a lamb. In the gospel story, Aries is not in a sacrificial position; it is the mature overcomer of Revelation 5 and 13:8. Like Gad, the lamb seemed to be overcome by the troop, but he overcame "at the last." Jewish tradition says Aries is a lamb, and its brightest star Hamal actually does mean lamb in Arabic so let's follow that train of thought. Lambs form flocks, faithfully following the shepherd. The Jewish people eventually realized that only the God of their ancestors would bring them the spiritual freedom they craved. They humbled themselves to acknowledge that the only possible way to leave Egypt would be with God's help.

They didn't have a lot of faith, but they were desperate, which was enough for them to follow God into the desert. They were like lambs that finally discovered the shepherd who cares for them. The exodus from Egypt took place in the month of the lamb, which was very significant. The blood of the lamb was used on the doorpost as protection from the destroyer, and Christians often plead the blood of Jesus (the symbolic lamb) for protection from evil.

In additional symbolism in the stars, the decans in Aries further the story, especially if you understood last month's Pieces. Aries is reaching a foot across the cords binding the fish to Cetus the sea monster, who might represent Leviathan. The ram is said to either be claiming the fish (God's people) as his or cutting the cords that bind them.

ניסן Nisan

Cassiopeia is the enthroned woman and is a picture of the church with the king at her side, handing her a scepter. But she sometimes suffers the indignity of being turned upside down.

As we mentioned, Cetus the sea monster is holding onto Pieces and threatening Andromeda the chained woman, but the last decan Perseus, the breaker of Andromeda's chains, comes in, sword brandished. Are you seeing the picture of freedom yet?

The gate that begins the year is the first gate that Nehemiah mentions that needed to be rebuilt. The Sheep Gate was believed to have been a gate in the eastern wall, near the pool of Bethesda.

"Then Eliashib the high priest arose with his brothers the priests and built the Sheep Gate; they consecrated it and hung its doors. They consecrated the wall to the Tower of the Hundred and the Tower of Hananel. Next to him the men of Jericho built, and next to them Zaccur the son of Imri built" (Nehemiah 3:1–2 NASB).

Eliashib means "God will restore." Zaccur means "remembered" or "mindful," which comes from the verb זכר (*zakar*), to cause to "remember or review—by means of public oration, urging and pleading." Imri means "my utterance."

In other words, "God will restore; he remembers my pleas and my utterance." As we begin a new cycle and look at our first gate, the Israelites had let go of some of the promises, and their place of peace was in ruins. But Nehemiah came repenting for what his generation and previous generations had done to cause Jerusalem's (place of peace) current predicament. We can always count on God to hear us and restore what he's given us. As Nehemiah began the work, the mockers and discouragers came around. You need not listen to the voices (internal or external) that scorn or try to intimidate you as you move forward. In John 10, Jesus actually says that he is the sheep gate. He was sharing a parable about how the shepherd comes in through the gate, but the thief only comes in over the wall. The sheep only listen to the shepherd. The first order of business for the high priest when building and consecrating the sheep gate is to consecrate our ear gates so that we only listen to and follow our Shepherd as we are in this new season and new cycle.

When God initiated Passover, he put Israel into a yearly cycle of redemption and commanded that Nisan now be the head of the months. (Originally, the Hebrew year started in the month of Tishri.) Passover starts at sundown on Nisan 15 and continues for seven days. If you would like to celebrate with a Seder meal, knock yourself out; I "pass over" that one. (Pun intended.)

Relevant flower essences are Horseradish (a traditional Passover bitter herb whose essence enables you to break away from where you've been), Trumpet Vine (speak out), Wild Rose (fight resignation), Wormwood (a bitter herb whose essence helps you leave the past behind), and Hyssop (an herb used to apply the blood; an essence for shame, guilt, and unworthiness). Horseradish and Lovage flower essences can help you step out into the unknown as you shake off the complacency that says, "I'll stay here because this is all I know."

The heart and intent of Passover is to celebrate God's goodness and faithfulness in extricating his people (you) from bondage. It's a time to look back and give thanks for what you've been delivered from. You are not where you used to be, am I right? You might not have arrived at your personal promised land yet, but he'll get you there the quickest way that you'll go.

To summarize this and apply it personally, list the areas where you feel trapped: emotional, financial, relational, etc. You might carve out some time on Rosh Chodesh and ask God what he wants to tell you/show you about this month. Declare out loud that freedom is coming to you and speak redemption over every circumstance. Say, "God, I receive all manner of miracles, healing, deliverance, and provision that you have for me at this time!" You might also prayerfully consider making some changes in the areas God shows you.

This is my Passover testimony from the first year when I started this. I didn't realize it was the first day of Passover. I was shopping at King's Discount Store, and I found a hyssop plant of all things. I use it, so I bought it. (The children of Israel used hyssop to paint the doorjamb on Passover.) I drove around with the plant all day and then was extremely emotionally wounded by someone later. I thought I was going to lose it. I put out a mass prayer request and the whole nine yards. I was trying to get home to my flower essences to stop this hurt while I could still think somewhat clearly and was declaring my mind covered by the blood. *Then* I realized it was Passover. My attention shifted, and I posed a big scary borderline-heretical question to God about how far I could run with a revelation I had about the blood. By the time I got home, I had a recorded message from a friend, prophesying the answer to that question, which confirmed everything I was too scared to think.

All that to say, I did not pick out this area to advance in when I thought of freedom from slavery. But I soooo got free. Not that day, not in Nisan, but in a process throughout the year. So do make your list of specific areas, but stay open to other possibilities, and watch what comes up around Passover. What buttons are being pushed? Those might be clues of what you need to leave behind.

We don't know exactly all that has to be orchestrated in our own personal exodus. Israel had the Abrahamic covenant. They were supposed to be a free nation, but they forgot their identity and wound up in bondage. I don't know why it took so long for God to create Moses, but he did; then he had to move Moses into the palace so that he would understand Egyptian government and process, move him back out before he became too entrenched in the life of a prince, move him into the desert where he could deal with his self-image problems, and eventually form him into a leader.

Nisan ניסן

Then were the ten plagues and a very hard time before the breakthrough, which left everybody with a tremendous amount of uncertainty and insecurity.

My point is, a process is certainly involved, and if we don't have the capacity to accept the needed change and do what we must do, then God will faithfully work on us until we can get there.

If you already know you're being led to take a certain step, but you've been putting it off, this is the time to act. If you've recently left something behind, yay, you're on the move! Life might feel a little harrowing right now, but look for the miracles, which will help you stay positive. You're on a necessary journey.

Nisan ניסן

Month at a Glance

Iyar אייר

Starts in April or May

Meaning: I am God, your healer

Blessing: Disease prevention

Area of Healing: Bitterness and unforgiveness

Action Needed: Listen to God. Get to know him better.

Warfare: Guard against distraction or being rattled by temporary circumstances

Tribe: Asher

Gem: Olivine/peridot

Gate: Fish

Constellation: Taurus the bull

Decans: Orion the mighty one, Eridanus the river, Auriga the shepherd

Iyar אייר

Iyar אייר

Last month, we were walking out of captivity and declaring ourselves free. What came up during Passover? The areas we identify are what we will be working through in the next five months. There is such a thing as walking it out, and oh, boy, are we there.

This month, we will develop greater sensitivity to hear Spirit, to be in tune and in timing, and to understand the secrets of God. We will also look at natural healing for physical issues, not just our emotions. We will look at where bitterness is in our lives and allow the sweetness to come in.

Iyar is also associated with light or radiance. Just as natural light and our day length increases, God wants to give us more and more revelation about ourselves and our circumstances. If you do nothing else this month, get to know God better by asking him to share about himself with you.

To follow the Hebraic calendar, we follow the journey of the Israelites. When they left Egypt, before they arrived at Sinai, they came to Mara, and they found the water there bitter. Moses was instructed to throw a tree into it, which miraculously made the water sweet. Then God taught them a lesson from it. "This isn't just about fixing water. If you listen to me, you won't have any of the diseases that the Egyptians have, for I am Jehovah Rapha, God your Healer." (Iyar is an acronym for "I am God, your healer" in Hebrew.) Notice he was speaking preventatively there.

Cancer in particular stems from bitter roots. I would imagine bitterness lets in more diseases than just cancer, however. Our emotional health is very closely tied with our physical health, and often, our internal bitterness is the result of our focus. We can choose to see the positives in a situation, or we can stew and complain. A powerful way to circumvent this is by recounting what he has done for us individually and continue finding his names. "The God who puts my puzzles together, the God who finds me parking spaces . . . . "

We can choose the Tree of the Knowledge of Good and Evil, or we can choose the Tree of Life. Which one is going in your water?

Plantain flower essence in particular helps transform bitterness. Bitterness does not have to be against another person the way we might usually think. The Israelites, whatever they might have been dealing with while they were grumbling against Moses, had traveled three days without water, only to find some that was undrinkable. In this case, life obstacles were the source of bitterness. We need to remember that whatever circumstances we find ourselves in, God has the power and the principles for transformation and will use them to get you to the next place on your journey. (After this, they came to Elim with twelve springs and palm trees.)

Self-heal flower essence helps your intuition in the area of healing. It helps you tune in and understand what you personally need to do for your health, so I would encourage you to pay attention to weird ideas that come to mind. Throw a tree in the water and that'll fix bitter water? Sounds ludicrous, right? Go out on a limb this month. Self-heal also helps with the motivation to do what you know you need to do to take care of yourself.

Manna began falling on the 15th of Iyar (Exodus 16:1–4), and Jewish tradition says that Iyar is a great time for digestive problems to be healed as well. This is because the Israelites were only eating manna at this time, which was the perfect food and which gave their digestive system a break.

As the story of Iyar continued, God began to reveal more and more of his personality and what he would do for his kids who, at that point, did not really know him. They began to learn his different names and how they connected to different attributes.

They had been slaves under a different rulership with its own gods. They didn't know much about this God who had just extricated them from Egypt. No matter where you are on the spectrum of knowing God, you can always learn more, and this is a significant month for that. This is the month where he wants to show and tell about himself, but you'll have to make the first move like Moses did and ask him. Side note: I've been noticing that I get answers quickly when I ask out loud.

Our gate of the month is the Fish Gate, where they brought the fish into Jerusalem (the city of peace). This was typically the noisiest and most crowded area of the city, and we might have to guard against distractions, and stay focused on our mission and being tuned to God's voice. As I've already mentioned, fish biblically represent human souls, so think in terms of bringing others into a place of peace as well.

"The Fish Gate was rebuilt by the sons of Hassenaah. They laid its beams and put its doors and bolts and bars in place. Meremoth son of Uriah, the son of Hakkoz, repaired the next section. Next to him Meshullam son of Berekiah, the son of Meshezabel, made repairs, and next to him Zadok son of Baana also made repairs." (Nehemiah 3:3-4).

If we look at the names and their meanings here, we see a theme of affliction and deliverance, and oh, there's our bitterness again.
Hassenaah: thorny, to prick
Meremoth: bitterness

Urijah: God is my light. (Iyar is associated with light.)
Koz: thorn
Meshullam: peace maker (Peace in the Hebrew world is not so much the absence of war, but wholeness, completeness, and harmony.)
Berechiah: blessed by Yah
Meshezabeel: God delivers
Zadok: righteous
Banna: affliction

We may have some blocks and defenses up that prevent us from hearing. One of those might be the image of a scary God from our upbringing in religion. We might subconsciously fear what he might say. We can use California Poppy and Angelica essences as a precautionary measure to find our own meaningful heart connection with God rather than going through a middle man or trying to navigate around the idea of true relationship entirely.

The constellation for this month is Taurus. Taurus seems to rise out of Aries the lamb's body and is stomping on Cetus the sea monster's head. In Greek mythology, the story goes that Jupiter loved Europa so much that he decided to change into the form of a bull just to be close to her. It worked. First, she petted him and then seated herself on his back. He then sprang away with her back to his home where he revealed his true self to her and won her love. Jesus loved the bride so much that he decided to change into the form of a human just to be close to

Iyar אייר

her. He is revealing his true self to her to win her love. This is a time of getting to know God.

The bull was also a sacrificial animal, and a castrated bull, known as an ox, was used for agricultural work. The Pleiades and Hyades are two star clusters within Taurus. On a more practical level, seasons were marked by their rising and setting. "But when the Pleiades and Hyades and strong Orion begin to set, then remember to plough in season." -Hesiod, Works and Days.

The decan Orion (who was known as a giant) is one of the most brilliant of all the constellations. Remember, Iyar is associated with radiance. The Sumerians called him Ur-ana, the light of heaven. The Babylonians knew Orion as the heavenly shepherd. Christian sources typically look at Orion as a hero with his lion head held up in triumph. However, Orion is in the Bible; the Hebrew word is *kesil* or "fool" (Proverbs 26; Job 9:9; 38:31; Amos 5:8). Some say this giant is Nimrod, who conspired against God (what a fool), and we have reason to believe he did so in the area of astrology. Orion in Greek mythology was a mighty hunter; Nimrod in the Bible was a mighty hunter before the Lord (Genesis 10:9). Ancient legends dating back to seventh-century Persia connect Nimrod with Orion and even call the constellation by his name. The idea of Taurus the bull charging at Nimrod makes more sense than if Orion were a hero and the personification of Christ. But some say that the meaning of Orion has nothing to do with the fool of Proverbs; instead the word comes from the

Babylonian word *kislimu*, when Orion is at its highest and brightest and that "fool" is a latter-day exegesis.

Eridanus the River is a huge constellation that comes from under Orion's foot. A legend about Nimrod says Abraham threw an egg at him in a dream that turned into a river and swept all his men away. River of fire and river of judgment are common Christian interpretations of the meaning of this river's name but are based on mistranslations of star names. However, while the name translations are suspect, I don't know that the premise is wrong. One theory says Eridanus comes from the name of a Babylonian constellation known as the Star of Eridu. Eridu was a Babylonian city held sacred to the god Enki-Ea. Enki-Ea was the ruler of the Abyss, usually imagined as a reservoir of water below the Earth's surface. The biblical abyss is a place for containing evil spirits until the lake of fire (Revelation 20:1-3). Luke 8:31 refers to it as "the deep." Cetus the sea monster is trying to stop its flow.

Auriga "the shepherd or charioteer (with no chariot)" has some bands in his hands and is holding a she-goat and two kids. The goat is clinging to his neck and looking down at Cetus in the river, whom she has presumably been saved from. All Christian interpretations that I have read have turned the goats into sheep and discussed how the sheep are saved by the shepherd. But I can't ignore that this constellation is very clearly goats (star name Capella means "she-goat"), and the Bible has never used sheep and goats interchangeably. I'll leave that up to your eschatology and interpretation.

The tribe is Asher, and his prophecy is, "out of Asher his bread shall be fat, and he shall yield royal dainties" (Genesis 49:20 KJV). Asher possessed the most fertile lands and had a thriving agricultural community. Again, plowing with Taurus is associated with this idea. The tribe of Asher supplied olive oil. The manna started in the month of Iyar, and Asher's "bread" would be fat. Manna is sometimes called the "bread of heaven" (Psalm 78:24) and was the Israelites' only sustenance. "He humbled you, causing you to hunger and then feeding you with manna, which neither you nor your ancestors had known, to teach you that man does not live on bread alone but on every word that comes from the mouth of the Lord." (Deuteronomy 8:3; Matthew 4:4; and Luke 4:4). It drives home the point that our lives can depend on our ability to hear from God. He is our sustenance.

Asher's flag was said to be "the color of an expensive jewel worn by women" and had an olive tree on it. This doesn't give us much to go on, although among Egyptians, the emerald was a status symbol. Cleopatra gave them to her dignitary friends. Olivine or peridot is a contender as I'm quite sure it was one of the original stones, readily available, and soft enough, unlike the actual emerald. Peridot is purported to be healing to bitterness (our theme of Iyar), resentment, and strife while promoting joy and confidence.

Another idea is that Asher's stone is amber. I initially fought the idea of amber as Asher's stone, since it technically isn't a gemstone; it's tree resin. Yet many researchers agree. I looked at where the tribe of Asher settled and who they are now. The Baltic region people are the supposed modern-day Asherites. And Baltic amber is world-renowned. I later came across an article saying that the reason the tree in the water removed the bitterness is because at every heavy mineral spring is a species of tree that produces sap that settles the minerals out of the water so that it becomes drinkable. While this takes some of the mystery out of the event, I find it very cool, because you don't have to know the science in order to participate in the natural cures. You just have to know God.

Iyar אייר

Month at a Glance
Sivan סיון

Starts in May or June

Meaning: Season or time

Blessing: Covenant

Area of Healing: Mental division and doublemindedness, internal conflict

Action Needed: Meet with God, set boundaries with others, take your inheritance

Warfare: Bind fear of deep spiritual experiences

Holidays: Shavout, Pentecost

Tribe: Benjamin

Gem: Rainbow jasper

Gate: Old Gate

Constellation: Gemini the twins

Decans: Lepus the hare, Canis Major the big dog, Canis Minor the little dog

Sivan סיון

Sivan סיון

We have a lot going on this month. We are completing some things and walking out what we declared during Nisan. We declared ourselves free of slavery or bondage, whatever that looks like for you. We had to exercise our muscles when it comes to trusting God, and this month, there is a major stopover to meet with God for further instructions.

Shavout begins on the evening of Sivan 6 and ends on the evening of Sivan 8. This is the anniversary of when God gave the Jews the Torah at Mt. Sinai. Judaism was basically born at this time, and really this season is about the covenant between God and his people. God acknowledged that even though all the nations were his, these people were set apart to be "a kingdom of priests and a holy nation." (Exodus 19:6)

On Pentecost, another covenant date, the people received the Holy Spirit, and the Christian church was born. This is a marked time for you to receive what God has for you. In both instances, the people that received were those waiting expectantly on those dates.

Receiving the law was a great thing; receiving the new covenant upgrade was an even better thing. How much more does the new covenant hold for you? You might have to find out!

Moses had to go up the mountain to meet with God, and he had to set some strong boundaries with the people so that he had that time alone. You might sense a spiritual change as other people around you might not be able to go where you are going in a metaphorical sense. God makes covenants with people groups but he's also very personal, and you'll need to have your own destiny journey and personal covenant with him. This doesn't mean that you won't share revelation with others, but God is probably going to give some insight to you alone. Motherwort flower essence can help you set those boundaries, and Wild Aztec Tobacco can deal with fear that keeps you closed off from spiritual experiences.

The sign associated with Sivan is Gemini the twins. There are two very bright stars in Gemini, which represent the twins, Castor and Pollux. The story varies, but Castor and Pollux had a mortal mother Leda and father Zeus. Castor was mortal, and Pollux was immortal. Castor dies, and Pollux was inconsolable, begging Zeus to relieve him of the bonds of immortality. Pollux chose death so that he could join his brother, and Zeus reunited them in the heavens as Gemini. They are said to help sailors in trouble, so keep that in mind for next month. As an aside, Paul actually sailed in a boat with their figures carved into it (Acts 28:11). He did not seem to be upset that his vessel was linked to astrological symbols.

So much is happening in this month. We can look at the Greek mythology in the zodiac metaphorically, because most of it seems to be a twisting of the truth. We can look at Castor and Pollux as the two sides of Jesus, both as the immortal son of God and part of the Trinity, and as the God who became mortal, born to a human woman, and who died for us out of love. We can also view Castor as us, and Pollux as Jesus, dying for us so we could be together forever in heaven. (Castor is actually six stars, by the way; six is the number of man.) The law that man could never live up to was given during this month, which adds an important contextual element to the twins.

Jacob and Esau are traditionally associated with Sivan. This is a great time to choose which inheritance we will take. We all have certain traits in our family trees that are positive and negative. At this time, we can be intentional about claiming those wonderful aspects we saw in our parents and grandparents or through our genealogy research, and we can renounce the less stellar qualities that we do not want to repeat.

Sivan סיון

During Sivan, the revelation hit me and my co-authors for the material that later became our book, *Accessing Your Spiritual Inheritance*. If you haven't gotten a copy of that yet, this is a great month to go through that process. So much generational work is fixated on the negative, but we should focus on the blessings that roll for one hundred generations down the line.

Rose Campion flower essence and the 528 Creative DNA essence may help you bring these things into focus. Be aware of any dreams with ancestors in them, release forgiveness for their participation in fear, anger, or other negative attributes, and declare you are breaking the cycle.

Our corresponding gate for the month is the Old Gate. "Stand at the crossroads and look; ask for the ancient paths, ask where the good way is, and walk in it, and you will find rest for your souls" (Jeremiah 6:16). Again, our purpose is to walk out of bondage and toward promises. The rubber is hitting the road, so to speak, even though you've been on the move before.

The literal Old Gate was a place where the elders gathered to help people solve problems. Joiada son of Paseah and Meshullam son of Besodeiah repaired the Old Gate (Nehemiah 3:6).

Let's look at the meanings of the names here:
Jehoiada: God knows
Paseah: Lame or limping

Sivan סיון

Meshullam: Peace maker, to make whole or complete
Besodeiah: Counsel of God

In other words, God knows when you're having trouble with your walk. He is your peace maker, ready to give counsel so that you can be whole.

Mullein flower essence seems to be particularly relevant to the Old Gate for hearing God about pathways, matters of conscience, and certainty in the way you should go.

The month also has some association with some doublemindedness. We can also have mood swings or some patterned divisive or conflicting thoughts. Kerria flower essence can help with this.

Our tribe of the month is Benjamin, and from the Midrash, his flag and therefore, the stone, had all the colors in it. Jasper comes in a wide range of hues, often in one stone. Rainbow jasper in particular is said to balance the mind, helping refine thought processes in order to work through issues. It is also said to help us work harmoniously with others.

When I was laying out the tribes with the months and looking at the prophecies and all the details to match them up with the right constellations, I did not know where to put Benjamin. He was the last one placed, and I was worried he was just sliding in by process of elimination and that he didn't really fit, that I had a mistake somewhere. Then I saw the decans in Gemini, the two Canis, and the wolves with Benjamin's banner, which has a wolf on it. I thought about his dualist prophecy and thought, *Yup, we can roll with this for Sivan.*

"Benjamin is a ravenous wolf; in the morning he devours the prey, in the evening he divides the plunder" (Genesis 49:27). The obvious association is that both these activities are warlike, and Benjamin was famous for their warfare. But we see a morning and evening marker here with two wolves in the sky, and devouring and dividing are very different activities. Similar, although not exactly the same, the loyalties of the tribe of Benjamin were always divided; they started a civil war.

I'm reminded of the Native American parable about two wolves fighting inside us. One is good; one is evil, and the one that you feed wins.

Month at a Glance

Tammuz תמוז

Starts in June or July

Meaning: Unknown, but named after a deity

Blessing: Practical revelation

Area of Healing: Negativity and fear responses

Action Needed: Watch your perceptions, let God be big

Warfare: Be vigilant against idolatry

Holidays: None

Tribe: Zebulon

Gem: Clear quartz

Gate: Valley Gate

Constellation: Cancer the crab

Decans: Ursa Major the big bear, Ursa Minor the little bear, Argo the ship

Tammuz תמוז

Tammuz תמוז

Tammuz marks the beginning of a new season. Right now, we need to go over prophetic promises for our lives so that we can step into them. This would be a great time to review dream journals and any other spiritual documentation you have. Can you take a step of faith at this time?

Our ability to see our circumstances in the right light is crucial this month. Queen Anne's Lace and Hawkweed flower essences go together to amplify your spiritual vision. Hawkweed is especially helpful when you're in the valley. What you see and the way that you see it will be important. This is about not only seeing prophetically but seeing the good in every situation and in every person, and Thimbleberry flower essence helps with that.

Tammuz contains the potential to be a time of enormous blessing. The trick here is to not forget your Source. This is a time to resist falling back into old belief systems or methods of coping. We have some choices to make this month, and while we always think we want more of God and want to break through our former boundaries, we also love control and familiarity. We would generally never admit it, but it's more comfortable for us to make him smaller than working on enlarging our capacity.

When we left off last month, Moses had gone up the mountain on the 7th of Sivan and was getting the Torah with the "do not cross" tape at the bottom. He had to spend the next forty days up there, receiving the full revelation.

The people waited, and due to a miscommunication, they thought he was due back on the 16th of Tammuz. When he didn't arrive according to their schedule, panic set in. They feared that they were suddenly leaderless and that Moses had probably burned to a crisp up there. Or as the Talmud put it, Satan showed them Moses in a vision, dead lying on a bier.

Their journey had been fueled by Moses's inspiration, vision, and the miracles he brought about. Without their leader, they felt doomed to die in the desert.

Moses had left Aaron in charge, and the people demanded that he make them a god to follow. They were used to a visual representation, something

Moses's God didn't comply with. In short, they defaulted to what they were comfortable with in the crisis.

In our lives, that can take on myriad forms. What is your default when circumstances look tough? What actions do you take when you lose your trust in your Source? I think I work harder. I might trust money to take care of me, so I do what's necessary to get more of it. We can also become a little too reliant on the people in our lives, especially any type of spiritual leader. During this month, more than ever, we have to hold fast to faith.

On the 17th of Tammuz, what should have been the ultimate paradigm shift and clear route to the promised land, was smashed into bits because of idolatry. Various patterns of idolatry have followed during Tammuz ever since. Does that mean we're in a bad month? No! But this is a month of challenge, confrontation, and extremes, and you cannot pick the middle of the road.

Our corresponding gate is the Valley Gate. The Valley Gate led to two important valleys in the Bible. The first was the Valley of Hinnom, where people offered their children to Mollech (idolatry). This valley was later called Gehenna in Greek. Hinnom was situated between Zion and the Hill of Evil Counsel. (Imagine that on a map in your mind for a minute.) The other valley is the Valley of Kidron, where idols were brought and destroyed.

Not much is said about those who repaired the Valley Gate. Hanun and the inhabitants of Zanoah worked on it. Hanun means "favored." According to *Strong's Concordance*, Zanoah means "rejected." Quite a stretch of wall is between the Old Gate and the Valley Gate. A lot of other workers were repairing along the wall, leading up to the Valley Gate. Their names represent what God did. Some of these include "whom Jah has delivered," "whom Jah has cured," "appointed by Jah," "thought of Jah," and "praised of Jah." This is the proper focus: to recount what God has done so that you can reject the Valley of Hinnom in favor of smashing idols in the Valley of Kidron.

This month, be acutely aware of any fear or negativity playing in your head. Yellow Monkey flower essence is helpful if you run into that. How we view our circumstances will determine whether we enter God's promises or wander through another cycle in the desert. Stop and use your spiritual sight to *see* what's really going on.

Okay, let's get down to business. The month of Tammuz is associated with the tribe of Zebulon, famed for success in business. They were seafaring merchants, and one of the decans in our star sign Cancer is also a ship. If you are in business, ask for spiritual downloads about how to more effectively do business. Many of us also need to heal our relationship with money so that it works for us. Star Thistle flower essence can help with a poverty mentality, and many of us probably wanted out of that captivity during Nisan.

Star Thistle also fights miserly tendencies when you don't feel like giving. Giving is a key factor this month, and you may want to reevaluate how and where you give. The Zebulon tribe in particular funded Issachar so they could put all their time into their education, studying the Torah rather than becoming side tracked with trying to make a living. In return, Zebulon then shared in Issachar's spiritual wealth. For our purposes, you might want to consider giving toward someone's spiritual education, which might be a scholarship fund or someone's tuition.

Moses said, "Rejoice, Zebulun, in your going forth, and Issachar, in your tents; They shall call peoples to the mountain; there they shall offer righteous sacrifices; for they shall draw out the abundance of the seas, and the hidden treasures of the sand" (Deuteronomy 33:18–19).

That's a perfect mirror of the natural and the spiritual of Issachar and Zebulon. Zebulon's international trade drew provision out of the seas so that Issachar could draw provision out of the spirit.

Zebulon's stone was either white or clear and commonly translated as diamond. We don't think it was actually a diamond; it was probably quartz. Quartz's ability to focus, amplify, and store and transform energy is used throughout the technology world in clocks, watches, radios, televisions, electronic games, computers, cell phones, electronic meters, and GPS equipment. Those qualities also apply in a more spiritual context. Think "even the rocks will cry out" (Luke 19:40) in terms of what happens if we fail or misdirect our worship. Quartz is said to raise our vibration as high as possible. Clear quartz also amplifies whatever intent is programmed into it and continues to carry or broadcast that energy. For this reason, I spiritually cleanse and pray over it, or let it sit with worship music for a while.

Cancer the crab draws out of the abundance of the seas and combs through the sand. Cancer might be the most changed from its original meaning, so it might not even be a crab. We don't have a Hebrew word for this constellation. Looking at star meanings, the constellation might have something to do with a pastoral setting with cattle-folds, sheepfolds, and two donkeys. I'm a bit leery of some of the methods of translation, however, but agree with the two donkeys. The beehive cluster of stars in Cancer is also called Praesepe, which means "the manger" in Latin. The main consensus is that it's a final resting place for the church.

Genesis 49:13 says Zebulon will be a haven (a safe harbor) for ships. I am speculating that that means they are a welcome port for other sea-faring nations. As I said previously, since so many different cultures have Cancer as a crab (an unclean creature), I prefer not to brush this symbolism aside and make it into something more pleasing. Peter had a vision of the unclean and recognized that the unclean symbolized meant Gentiles are accepted too (Acts 10). The crab is a creature born of water as is the church with many legs. If they are correct in the translations of sheepfolds, Jesus did say that he had other sheep not of this fold (John 10:16). Marketplace ministry will bring other sheep into this fold. ".They will summon peoples to the mountain and there offer the sacrifices of the righteous; they will feast on the abundance of the seas, on the treasures hidden in the sand."(Deuteronomy 33:19)

For a recap, keep looking up to see the best if you are in the valley. Look for business strategies from the right source rather than your own efforts or partnering with the enemy, and try to let God be big.

Tammuz תמוז

Month at a Glance

Starts in July or August

Meaning: Father

Blessing: Sonship, Father's promises

Area of Healing: Father wounds, self-worth

Action Needed: Be bold in going after the promise

Warfare: Guard against listening to bad counsel

Holidays: 9th of Av

Tribe: Judah

Gem: Blue Chalcedony

Gate: Dung Gate

Constellation: Leo the lion

Decans: Hydra the serpent, Crater the cup, Corvus the raven

אב Av

אב Av

We started last month by talking about seeing things correctly, and this month is a continuation of that with a slightly different spin.
It's Av, and if you know much about it, or run with people who do, this month is usually preceded by nervousness and hand-wringing. We aren't going to go there. When I was attempting to write and research, I kept falling asleep and having dreams that made it clear to not address the negatives but to focus instead on what we need to understand this month.

There are three things I believe you are supposed to "get" this month. First, you are enough. More than enough. You have been thoroughly prepared, and everything you need is present to step into that place you've been working toward. All the things about you that make you "you," even some things you might consider a liability, are what position you to overcome your obstacles. Buttercup, Aurinia, and Elecampane are helpful flower essence backups to address this mindset this month.

The second is your spiritual hearing. You need a strong connection in order to take some serious ground this month. Your intuition needs to be fully functional.

The third is healing your relationship with your father. The name Av literally means "father." Most people didn't have perfect fathers; I had a pretty good one and still went through some healing on Sunflower essence. If you are not healed in this area, you tend to have a distorted perception of God as a father. This can cause you to shut down your spiritual hearing. "La la la, I don't want to listen to you." Even on a subconscious level, you can rebel if you had a strict, angry, or uninvolved dad.

When I was coming out of my first Av dream before I wrote this, "Father Figure," a song by George Michael, was playing in my head. If you know it, the chorus fits the month.

Okay, so let me back up and unpack this a little further. The original problem with the 9th of Av was that during Tammuz, twelve spies, one from each tribe, were sent to check out the promised land. I don't know why they were called spies; it sounds very espionagey. I'd say they were actually scouts. They were supposed to find out the practical details of moving into the promised land: what the geography was, was it farmable, the best access routes, etc. God set them up in every way to succeed. Their assignment was to find out how to conquer the territory, but somewhere in the midst of their assignment, they began asking should we or shouldn't we rather than exactly how to accomplish the takeover.

So when the spies came back on the 9th of Av, two of them were super excited about enormous fruit and abundant resources while the other ten were intimidated by the giants living there. The ten convinced the people that waited behind that entering the promised land was not a good idea and that God and Moses were the bad guys for bringing them there. They wished they had stayed slaves.

Meanwhile, the two spies that were trusting that God would help them were trying to build faith into the people—faith that God was with them and had brought them to this place for a purpose, not just to die. Instead, the people threatened to stone them.

God's response was that if they didn't want to go to the promised land, they didn't have to go. They could stay in the desert for the rest of their lives. So that's what they did. He took care of them there, but it was far from the best that he had for them. The next generation and the two spies were the only ones who entered the land.

Now let's take another look at Nisan and personalize what happened. When you were declaring yourself free during Nisan, what was it from? What were you hoping to move toward? Do you see yourself on the cusp of that now? What are some things that intimidate you? What obstacles are you facing? In light of what I just said, how will you respond?

There's a critical point in transitioning from slaves to sons. It's a mindset of learning that in any situation that God puts you in or asks of you, you already have everything you need at the ready. It just doesn't look like it.

I don't know if this is to put one over on the enemy or to grow us in relationship and faith or both. When we are facing something that seems overwhelming and when it looks like you don't have what you need, ask what you've overlooked. "What resources am I not using that would apply to this situation?"

Listen, we have got to push through. Many tragedies have happened to the Jewish people on the 9th of Av. It's as if this one historical event of inferiority complex, lack of faith, and a belief that God set them up to fail opened a door to future devastation on the same date for centuries to come. Let's be courageous. Borage and Aurinia flower essences will help you pursue all God has for you.

I was grocery shopping the second day I tried to write this, and when I was checking out, I couldn't find the twenty dollars I thought I had put in my pocket. Later at home, while writing, an angel came and placed a twenty dollar bill next to me. In that instant, every memory of twenty that had come up over the past couple days rushed into my mind, and I knew it was more significant than "Hey, here's that twenty you were missing."

So I dug into the significance of the number twenty. In Hebrew, twenty is the letter *caph*, which means "to seize and hold." According to several examples in Hebrew text, it also means a complete waiting period. Jacob waited twenty years for possession; (Genesis 31:38, 41) Israel waited twenty years for deliverance. (Judges 4:3) This is just more confirmation that the time is now. It may be like that that instance of mine; one minute you don't have it, and then it miraculously is handed to you. Seize the month!

The ten in the above story were the naysayers, the play-it-safers, who dissuaded an entire nation from reaching the dream. You're going to need to resolve to be unstoppable and not let other people's doubts get in your head. Bonus points for sticking tightly to encouragers and/or those who are doing what you want to do. Go it alone if you have to, but go. It's your appointed time to conquer a new area. You've got this!

Leo the lion of the tribe of Judah is the constellation and tribe this month. Leo is treading on Hydra the serpent. Crater the cup is pouring out wrath on Hydra, and Corvus the raven is grasping Hydra with his claws and pecking him. The brightest star is Leo's heart. Its name is *regulus*, which means "little king" or "prince" in Latin. The star's Greek name, *Basiliscos*, has the same meaning.

Judah's prophecy from Jacob was this:

> Judah,[a] your brothers will praise you: your hand will be on the neck of your enemies; your father's sons will bow down to you. You are a lion's cub, Judah; you return from the prey, my son. Like a lion he crouches and lies down, like a lioness—who dares to rouse him? The scepter will not depart from Judah, nor the ruler's staff from between his feet, until he to whom it belongs shall come and the obedience of the nations shall be his. He will tether his donkey to a vine, his colt to the choicest branch; he will wash his garments in wine, his robes in the blood of grapes. His eyes will be darker than wine, his teeth whiter than milk. (Genesis 49:8–12).

You can see the repetition of the theme of overcoming and getting the choicest fruit. A lion won't back down this month or any time, and neither should you. The Lion of the tribe of Judah is standing with you. Who can be against you?

Judah's flag was "blue like skies," and therefore, the stone might have been blue chalcedony. Blue chalcedony is said to help us assimilate new ideas and accept new situations. It also helps those who tend to worry by helping them not to project into an imaginary future.

The decans, the star names, Judah's prophecy, and Jeremiah 25:15–38 all fit seamlessly with each other. Let's summarize the passage in Jeremiah right here. God said to Jeremiah to give a cup filled with the "wine of my wrath" to all the wicked nations. Remember the Crater the cup constellation? Jeremiah 25:30 says "The Lord will roar from on high; he will thunder from his holy dwelling and roar mightily against his land. He will shout like those who tread the grapes, shout against all who live on the earth." Skipping to 25:38, "Like a lion he will leave his lair, and their land will become desolate."

Our gate of the month is the Dung Gate or Potsherd Gate. All the garbage was taken out through this gate. Time to get rid of the crap before you move on to the Fountain Gate! We've talked about the false report earlier here. Malchiah, "the Lord is my counselor," was the repairer of the Dung Gate. Who you're listening to will be important.

א ב

Month at a Glance
Elul אלול

Starts in August or September

Meaning: I am my beloved's, my beloved is mine.

Blessing: God's presence

Area of Healing: Rejection, isolation, spiritual vision

Action Needed: Work on relational connections

Warfare: Don't jump through religious hoops or buy into unworthiness

Holidays: None

Tribe: Naphtali

Gem: Amethyst

Gate: Fountain Gate

Constellation: Virgo the virgin

Decans: Coma the desired one, Centaurus the centaur, Bootes the herdsman

אלול Elul

Elul אלול

"I am my beloved's and my beloved is mine." Elul is an acronym for that phrase from Song of Solomon 6:3 and sets our tone for the month. This beautiful and romantic sentence represents our relationship with Creator, which is often paralleled as a bride and groom. We switch gears this month, enjoy Gods presence, and heal from relational issues.

Elul is the time of the year when we can mostly easily sense God's closeness to us. It's as though the walls that we put up ourselves via poor judgments, fear, and pain, can be set aside. In this month, God meets us where we are.

Jewish texts relate this time as when "the king is in the field." According to the parable, for most of the year, the king is in a palace. To see or speak with him, you have to journey there, dress right, talk right, jump through all the hoops, and even then, only a select few are granted permission to enter. But at certain times, the king would go out among the people and set up a tent in a field where he was accessible to all. Anyone could go as they were and be received. At the end, the people escorted the king back to the palace, but this time they were not shut out. Through relationship built in the field, they now had access to the throne. As you know, we have access via Jesus whenever we want and wherever we are. The King met us once and for all where we are. This season stands as one of intimacy and restoration.

Elul is a month of strengthening connections with God and each other. Assuming an attitude of gratitude is a way of strengthening any connection. One of the possible pitfalls this month is mistrust and disconnection. Watch and fight the tendency to isolate. This is generally rooted in rejection. Malva and Oregon Grape essences can help, but as soon as you recognize this happening, take your pain to God and move back into gratitude. This is a time to mend fences and make things right between you and God or you and other people. When your buttons are pushed by people close to you, God is likely bringing things to the surface for healing if you'll choose to see it that way.

The tribe of the month is Naphtali. Prophecies for Naphtali are that he is like a doe set free. (See Genesis 49:21.) Naphtali means "my wrestlings." When God sets us free from our wrestlings, it's wonderful. This is also a time to receive strategies, answers, and insights. Make a point of asking questions.

Elul is when Moses went to see God and learned all about his mercy. He obtained God's forgiveness and reconciliation with the people. This is an opportune time for introspection and repentance. This is a time to take stock of the year before heading into Rosh Hashanah: what worked well, what didn't, and how we need to improve.

It's also time to develop our visions, prayers, and hopes for the new year. I've been impressed to write up a vision statement for the kind of person I want to be. This can be just a paragraph or two, defining the character and attributes I want to see in myself. This exercise carries no guilt or shame but is just a way to aspire higher.

As you might have noticed by now, the Hebrew year includes lots of beginnings, and we're at another one: the beginning of the zodiac. We start with Virgo the virgin with her wheat (the seed) in one hand and the branch (the messiah) in the other.

The gate of the month is the Fountain Gate, which was in the worst shape after the attack in Nehemiah. This tells me we really need Elul after going through Tevet and Av, or the Dung Gate and the Valley Gate. The symbolism of the fountain speaks of the living water, Holy Spirit, and refreshing. Soaking sessions might be in order.

אלול Elul

Solomon's garden was accessed through the Fountain Gate. " "You are a garden locked up, my sister, my bride; you are a spring enclosed, a sealed fountain.Your plants are an orchard of pomegranates with choice fruits, with henna and nard,nard and saffron,calamus and cinnamon, with every kind of incense tree, with myrrh and aloes and all the finest spices.You are a garden fountain,a well of flowing water streaming down from Lebanon" (Song of Songs 4:12–15.) It's another example of intimacy being restored. As an interesting aside, all gates and the wall were completed on the 25th of Elul.

"But the gate of the fountain repaired Shallun the son of Colhozeh, the ruler of part of Mizpah; he built it, and covered it, and set up the doors thereof, the locks thereof, and the bars thereof, and the wall of the pool of Siloam by the king's garden, and unto the stairs that go down from the city of David" (Nehemiah 3:15 KJV)

The word for fountain in this verse is *ayin* meaning "eye." The blind man's sight was restored when he washed in the pool of Siloam, mentioned in the verse above. (See reference.) This is a month to have your spiritual sight cleansed, especially after the toll of the previous two months. The Testament of Naphtali had a few things to say about the eye, one of which was "as his eye, so is his sleep." I take this to mean that spiritually cleaning your eye gates will help reduce nightmares.

Shallun means "retribution, to make whole or complete, to prosper."
Colhozeh means "seeing the whole."
Mizpah means "watchtower."

This sounds like a theme of restoring one's ability to see from a higher perspective and to see the whole picture. Watchtowers generally indicate a "watchman" or intercessory function.

Key flower essences for this month are Aurinia and Indian Pipe, connecting with the presence of God and building trust. Other helpful essences follow:
Harebell is for receiving God's love and letting love flow freely to others.
Hyssop helps with letting go of guilt/shame (since we're heading into introspection).
Russian Sage promotes gratitude, love, and joy.
Malva is for healing rejection.
Oregon Grape helps with healing distrust and seeing the good intentions of others.

Naphtali's stone, according to the Midrash, was "like wine that isn't too strong" and was very likely amethyst. Interestingly, amethyst has long been associated with sobriety. *Amethystos* in Greek means "not drunken." We have an Amethyst essence at Freedom Flowers that we've determined brings a sense of peace, calmness, and unusual contentment.

אלול Elul

Month at a Glance
Tishrei תשרי

Starts in September or October

Meaning: Head of the year

Blessing: Promotion

Area of Healing: Performance mentality

Action Needed: Reflection and gratitude

Warfare: Don't get caught up in focusing on sin

Holidays: Rosh Hashanah, Yom Kippur, Sukkot

Tribe: Levi

Gem: Sardonyx

Gate: Water Gate

Constellation: Libra the scales

Decans: Crux the cross, Lupus the victim, Corona the crown

Tishrei תשרי

Tishrei תשרי

Hey, it's the seventh month in the cycle and the Jewish New Year! I know, I know, confusing, but Nisan is the first month, and Tishri begins the "head of the year." Things are completing, and things are beginning. This month seems to find most of its identity from all the holidays. The whole month has something going on.

Rosh Hashanah begins at sundown on the last day of Elul and ends at nightfall on Tishri 3. One of the most significant observations of the holiday is the sounding of the shofar. A total of one hundred notes are sounded each day. We made a sound essence from the shofar so that even if you're not within earshot, you're still benefitting from that frequency. As with the regular Gregorian New Year, this is a time for reflection and review. This shofar essence called Awakening shakes you out of your status quo

Tishrei תשרי

and brings clarity about what needs to change. Trumpet also symbolizes a message or word given, so expect to receive revelation this month.

The Ten Days of Awe occupy the space between Rosh Hashanah and Yom Kippur. This is traditionally a time of continued introspection and repentance. It's a last-chance opportunity to repent and do right before your fate is sealed on Yom Kippur.

Yom Kippur begins the evening of the 10th and is considered one of the most solemn and holy days in the Jewish calendar. According to tradition, God writes the names of who will live and who will die in that year and seals the verdict on Yom Kippur. Let's tip the Days of Awe by being in awe that we can rest from our efforts to be accepted by God, that our works cannot save us. Repentance is always beneficial, but let's use this seventh month of the year as a Sabbath, a denying of religious labor. Instead of praying for mercy, we can be thankful we already have it.

I do believe God is making weighty decisions during this time. I have noticed that the positions of people change in the fall months. In fact, students move to a new grade in school every fall. In an organization I belonged to, we unknowingly had this pattern of looking at everybody around September of every year to see who we could reposition. We looked at their gifts and abilities and tried to move them into an area that would be more fulfilling to them as well as more beneficial to the whole group. We weren't looking at their faults; we were finding the gold and trying to put them in places they would shine. And we certainly weren't paying attention to the Jewish calendar when we did this.

This experience has me thinking that God is doing the same thing, only better. I believe he is always looking for ways to promote us and will push us forward in any area he can. You may have been a screw up in some areas this year. That doesn't matter. There's still greatness in you that he will work with.

The constellation is Libra; the scales symbolize justice and the price Jesus paid. The constellations around Libra tell a fuller picture as Corona (or crown of thorns) is nearby, along with Crux (the cross). Lupus the victim is dying at Ara the altar. The Babylonians thought that Lupus was not a wolf but a half man, half lion.

The tribe associated with Tishri is Levi. This tribe was given the responsibility to handle the items in the tabernacle and to minister to the nation. They were tasked with bringing balance and justice in the old covenant. Levi's stone might have been the sardonyx. The flag was said to have red, white, and black bands, and sardonyx (sard plus onyx in layers) fits. Jewelers create cameos from sardonyx. The white layer is carved away, leaving a facial relief against a red setting. Sardonyx is said to bring happiness and stability in relationships and improve integrity, strength of character, and discipline.

Tishrei תשרי

Our gate of the month is the Water Gate. This area was repaired by the Tekoites. Tekoa means trumpet. How fitting that the trumpeters worked on the gate that happens to correspond to Rosh Hashanah. On Rosh Hashanah, six days after the wall and gates were restored, the Jews had a gathering at the Water Gate, and the books were opened. (See Nehemiah 8.) This can represent understanding and enlightenment. Ezra read to the people from sunup to noon every day for seven days at the Water Gate. Last month, the focus was on our eyes. This month, our hearing is receiving a cleansing with the washing of the water of the Word. The Levites read from the book of the law of God, making it clear and giving meaning so that the people understood what was being read. People were repenting and weeping over their sin, and several times, both Nehemiah and the Levites had to tell the people not to grieve and to be joyous. We need to remember this as we go into the introspective Days of Awe.

Sukkot, or the Feast of Tabernacles, starts the evening of Tishri 14 and lasts a week. Traditionally, you build a hut to remember the fact that the Jews did not have permanency. In spite of this, it's somehow the most joyful of all the festivals. The people of Israel were actually instructed to use their tithe to buy food, wine, strong drink, or whatever their heart desired! (Deuteronomy 14:25–26). Party! This is a marked time to experience God's glory.

As far as flower essences go, Awakening is our sound essence made from shofar blasts. Otherwise, we

Tishrei תשרי

focus on joy this month with Zinnia, Russian Sage, Bee Balm, and Parrot Tulip.

Tishrei תשרי

Month at a Glance
Cheshvan חשון

Starts in October or November

Meaning: Eighth month

Blessing: Rest and transition

Area of Healing: Moving into new identity

Action Needed: Let go of old identity

Warfare: Fight against obstacles to your call

Holidays: None

Tribe: Dan

Gem: Turquoise

Gate: Horse Gate

Constellation: Scorpio the scorpion

Decans: Serpens the snake, Ophichus the serpent wrestler, Hercules the mighty one

חשון Cheshvan

Cheshvan חשון

Think of Cheshvan as a month off. It's down time to reflect, regroup, and settle into a rhythm of life after possibly switching gears in the last two months. Does your train feel like it's found new tracks? Some things undoubtedly came to a close during Tishri, which might continue in Cheshvan as well. I have faith that we all shifted into some new areas, and we need time to stabilize and integrate the new. Shasta Daisy flower essence can help us see the big picture and understand how all the pieces fit together after Tishri's eventfulness.

Let's assimilate everything we just gained and find our feet. Rest doesn't mean an absence of activity, but I sense we need to reevaluate what we are doing. Let's make sure we are involved in activities with a connection to the future and balance these with our daily living. Purple Archangel and Teasel flower essences can help with this.

During Cheshvan, the messiah is supposed to rebuild the temple. If you believe Jesus is the messiah, you are the temple, so don't be surprised if a rebuilding is going on within.

Otherwise, Cheshvan can feel pretty anti-climactic after Tishri, but this time is important for sustainable growth. A good analogy can be seen in the fall deciduous trees. The leaves drop and enter a barren season in which it appears nothing is happening. But below the surface, roots are growing deeper and stronger for the next season. We need to embrace this transition, this lull, the bleakness . . . .

Resist the need to shake things up and use the downtime to rest for the kind of work that will be fruitful in the future. You might continue to deal with root issues as well. Anything in the past that creates unhealthy mindsets can potentially stunt growth in the new season. These are typically distortions in the way we see ourselves, especially since we might have just undergone a change. Our identity may possibly be wrapped up in where we just were.

We may also continue to challenge conclusions we came to in early childhood about who we are. Black-eyed Susan flower essence can give us the courage to go deep within to the dark places and bring out hidden issues for healing. Missouri Primrose is a favorite for its ability to work on our sense of self-worth and help us feel worthy of our blessings. With all this talk about trees, we also need a tree essence. White Chestnut will help contribute to our quiet, introspective state. I'm hopeful for a period of deep revelation.

The constellation is Scorpio. It has other serpent-related constellations around it, and we're supposed to be treading on those. It is near the constellation Serpens, the serpent, and Ophiuchus, the snake holder. Scorpio used to be significantly larger, and in the first century, his claws became Libra's scales. The word for scorpion (from Arabic), *aqerab*, appears to be blended from the Hebrew *aqar*, "to wound," and the Hebrew *aqab*, which means "the heel."

"I will put enmity between you and the woman,
And between your seed and her seed;
He shall crush your head,
And you shall crush his heel" (Genesis 3:15).

Ophiuchus the snake holder is standing on the heart of Scorpio, and the stinger is at his heel. "They will pick up serpents, and if they drink any deadly poison, it will not hurt them; they will lay hands on the sick, and they will recover" (Mark 16:18 NASB.)

Hercules (the constellation predates any association with the Greek god) is kneeling and clubbing a fist full of snakes, and his foot is on the head of Draco. Hercules has been passed off as a type of Christ here, and as he is the son of a god who became mortal and had to grow up on earth, this makes sense. I also can't help but see the similarities between Hercules and Samson, a famous Dannite, our tribe of the month. (See Judges 13) Some Christians view Samson as a type and shadow of Jesus.

The tribe of the month is Dan. Dan's prophecy follows. "Dan shall be a serpent by the way, an adder in the path that biteth the horse heels, so that his rider shall fall backward" (Genesis 49:17 KJV.) Lovely, right? Serpents and wounded heels all over again. Dan's stone might have been turquoise, which was mined in Egypt and a favorite carving stone there. His banner indicates a bluish background. For centuries, turquoise has had a reputation of protecting riders from injuries if they fell off their horses. While this seems superstitious to me, I can't help wondering if it's from a known connection to the tribe of Dan. Turquoise supposedly helps overcome writer's block and is a stone of clear communication. It's especially good for those who work in law enforcement or in government. It also fights a martyr attitude and self-sabotage.

The eighth gate for the eighth month is the Horse Gate. Horses were a symbol of warfare and also of power and authority. Apparently, you had to get off your high horse to go through the gate. In many places in the Bible, God speaks negatively about people who trust in horses and chariots, pertaining to warfare, rather than in the counsel of God.

"Woe to those who go down to Egypt for help And rely on horses, And trust in chariots because they are many And in horsemen because they are very strong, But they do not look to the Holy One of Israel, nor seek the Lord!" (Isaiah 31:1).

"Some boast in chariots and some in horses, But we will boast in the name of the Lord, our God" (Psalm 20:7).

"A horse is a false hope for victory; Nor does it deliver anyone by its great strength" (Psalm 33:17).

"The horse is prepared for the day of battle, But victory belongs to the Lord" (Proverbs 21:31).

"With you I shatter the horse and his rider, And with you I shatter the chariot and its rider" (Jeremiah 51:21).

"They will be as mighty men, Treading down the enemy in the mire of the streets in battle; And they will fight, for the Lord will be with them; And the riders on horses will be put to shame" (Zechariah 10:5).

As a reminder, Dan's prophecy addresses being an adder in the path that bites the horse's heels, causing the rider to fall backward. So let's be aware that as we are moving into new areas, we might encounter some traps. Specifically, throughout the Bible, the word "scorpion" is used as a metaphor, referring to wicked or evil people who try to stop the call of God. We need to remember not to rely on our natural methods. We are not fighting a natural enemy, so we need to stay in our spiritual authority.

Remember that it's under your feet. St. John's Wort flower essence (different from the herbal supplement) can be helpful for walking in your authority.

Month at a Glance
Kislev כסלו

Starts in November or December

Meaning: Trust, hope

Blessing: Sleep and dreams

Area of Healing: Trust issues with God

Action Needed: Let whatever amount of light you have shine

Warfare: War against darkness from a place of rest

Holidays: Hanukkah

Tribe: Joseph

Gem: Black onyx

Gate: East Gate

Constellation: Sagittarius the archer

Decans: Lyra the harp, Ara the altar, Draco the dragon

כסלו Kislev

Kislev כסלו

Wow, where to begin? I'm looking forward to Kislev, even though it's a dark month. It's the month of dreams—night dreams—and we have a month of long nights for dreaming.

The spiritual sense associated with Kislev is sleep, and we need to work out any sleep issues in order to dream. I like White Chestnut flower essence as a sleep aid because it calms the mind, and even when I dream and wake up, it helps me stay out of the analytical mindset that "I have to solve this one right now." I can go back to sleep and keep dreaming. We do, however, want to watch and deal with what comes up in the night.

Kislev means "trust" and "hope." Trust and a sense of security is necessary to be able to sleep peacefully, to know that you are safe and looked after, that all your worries can be handed over. White Chestnut again is helpful here. Borage also is my main go-to essence for optimism and hope. This is a time to deal with any trust issues we have with God or others.

Often what's happening in the natural is mirrored in the spiritual. The days are getting shorter; the darkness is increasing, but that's not a bad thing. It's time for night vision, to go into the deep places and come out on the other side. People might commonly feel distant from God, as if they are in a place or a season where they don't necessarily sense his presence on a level that they have in the past. They might see him at work in their lives, but it's more of a faith walk rather than feeling as if they are brimming with evidence. Trust and hope are definitely in play.

Sweet Chestnut is relevant to those who are in a dark night of the soul, feeling hopeless or cut off from God. Because these feelings exist on a spectrum, this essence is still helpful with low-level feelings of being lost as well as extreme feelings of depression. St. John's Wort also has a long history of helping people face and overcome darkness.

We hardly associate rainbows with the shortest days of the year, but Noah departed the ark at the end of Cheshvan. This would not have been a positive time to start fresh and seed new crops; no, it must have been total desolation. On the first day of Kislev, God blessed Noah and his family and gave him new insights. According to the book of Jubilees, he sent an angel to teach Noah every kind of medicine to counter the spirits that would try to afflict them. Humankind would develop differently and become its own rainbow of color, sourced from pure white light, refracting into different shades.

And as the month becomes darker, here comes Hanukah, the Festival of Lights. In terms of the historical narrative of Hanukkah, the Hasmoneans stood up to their oppressors. Despite the darkness they were facing, they had faith for the miraculous. Then God opened their eyes to find a small measure of oil with which to kindle the menorah. That little bit of oil lasted eight days.

At the time, a significant number of Jewish people had crossed over into Hellenism, lovers of all things Greek. Hellenism found the concepts of spirituality, morality, and godliness to be threatening and dangerous. They outlawed the Torah because it took the mind to places beyond their Greek thinking. They instead attempted to force idol worship.

Then the miracle happened. The Greeks had defiled the menorah, which is a symbol of the spirit, just as they defiled everything else in the Temple. When the Temple was recaptured, one of the first things the fighters did was to try to rekindle the menorah. Lighting the menorah was a symbol of spiritual renewal. At a glance, the battle appeared to be over culture and politics, but it wasn't about political independence or maintaining culture then, and it shouldn't be now.

Each of us has to fight off darkness in our own way. We need to find our own tiny jar of oil in the darkness, light what we have, and let God extend the glow.

Our gate of the month is the East Gate. This one with double doors (double blessing) needed no repair. This is significant for us as we have journeyed through some difficult stuff over the past year. Jesus entered and exited the East Gate frequently in the week prior to the crucifixion as it leads out to the Mount of Olives. We have died to some things over the last several months. The symbolism of sleeping and waking is also a reminder of death and resurrection.

Dr. Adonijah Ogbonnaya (Dr O.) says the 713 frequency is the resurrection frequency. He says it "tunes creation back into its relationship with God, and your body to get health, strength, and power. It reorders perception and recalibrates the codes of body, soul, and spirit." We need to go beyond the cross and take part in the resurrection life beyond the veil. The 713 essence also aids in restful sleep with dreams.

Sagittarius the archer is our constellation. He is aiming his bow into the heart of Scorpio. The archer relates with the theme of Hanukah as the archer's bow of the Maccabees. Draco the dragon, who looks more serpent-like, is said to be the dragon who guards the golden apples of immortality in the Garden of the Hesperides. This is potentially a corruption of the Eden story. Last month, Hercules stepped on his head, and God said to Satan after turning him into a snake that the seed of the woman would bruise his head (Genesis 3:15). Jesus is giving us back access to the garden, to the pre-fall era, to immortality.

The tribe of the month is Joseph, which technically is not a tribe. When Joseph is referred to, it means Ephraim and Manasseh, or the "house of Joseph," which includes both. Joseph the dreamer received a double blessing. (Note again the connection with dreams.)

> Joseph is a fruitful vine, a fruitful vine near a spring, whose branches climb over a wall. With bitterness *archers attacked him; they shot at him with hostility. But his bow remained steady*, his strong arms stayed limber, because of the hand of the Mighty One of Jacob, because of the Shepherd, the Rock of Israel, because of your father's God, who helps you, because of the Almighty, who blesses you with blessings of the heavens above, blessings of the deep that lies below, blessings of the breast and womb. Your father's blessings are greater than the blessings of the ancient mountains, than the bounty of the age-old hills. Let all these rest on the head of Joseph, on the brow of the prince among his brothers (Genesis 49:22–26, emphasis added).

Joseph's stone might have been the black onyx as his banner was black. This is so appropriate for our dark month. Black onyx is said to help us access higher guidance and heal old grief and sorrow.

This is our month to war from a place of rest and to draw back so that we can hit the target with precision.

Sleep deep and dream well. You'll need it for Tevet.

Month at a Glance
Tevet טבת

Starts in December or January

Meaning: Good

Blessing: Seeing what we couldn't before

Area of Healing: Anger, victimization, judgment

Action Needed: Look from a higher perspective

Warfare: Bind any demonic influence that allows anger to color your perception

Holidays: Hanukah ends

Tribe: Simeon

Gem: Chrysoprase

Gate: Miphkad

Constellation: Capricorn the sea goat

Decans: Saggita the arrow, Aquilla the eagle, Delphinus the dolphin

Tevet טבת

Tevet טבת

In a nutshell, this month's healing focus is on letting go of anger, seeing things in the right light, and possibly doing some physical cleansing as well. The origin of this month's name is from Babylon. In Akkadian, the name is *Tabito*, which means something that you sink into, like mud. (We'll get to how the Babylonians relate to all this later.) On the other hand, *Tevet* also comes from the Hebrew word *tov*, meaning "good." There is very much an aspect of "which way ya gonna go" to the month.

Tevet is an ayin month in that it is the letter associated with Tevet. Ayin means to "look and look again" and also to "let your good eye see." Tevet is a time when we can see what we could not before. We can see what needs to be done; we can see new strategies, new paths to freedom. Hawkweed flower essence helps our vision go higher in the area of destiny.

We need the eyes of our understanding to be enlightened with the truth, to see the best and the potential in others, our circumstances, and ourselves. When we do see evil, we need to stand against it with prayer and words of life. This is a time when we can more easily see past our anger, frustration, and judgment toward others as well as ourselves. Some of us are also a little angry at God for where we are and what we continue to deal with. Horseradish flower essence helps us abandon any kind of victim mentality and realize we are not stuck; we are not sinking in the mud. Verbena aids us with dumping a critical spirit, and Milk Thistle is great for long-standing anger issues. Skullcap helps us forgive ourselves.

As anger, victimization, frustration, and judgments come up, we need to stop and really look at what's going on. Are we creating a scapegoat and passing blame? If you are having an issue with someone, are those traits in some way a part of your shadow that you don't like? Often what really bothers us about others is also true of ourselves.

Are we accepting the role of the scapegoat in our family, work, or other close community? If you are an empath, feeler, or sensitive person, you are especially vulnerable to taking on other people's junk. As you mirror that back to them, you might find yourself ostracized because they don't want to look at or deal with it.

Tevet טבת

The tribe associated with Tevet is Simeon. Moses didn't bless Simeon like he did the other tribes. Jacob's prophecy was that " "their swords are weapons of violence. Let me not enter their council, let me not join their assembly for they have killed men in their anger and hamstrung oxen as they pleased. Cursed be their anger, so fierce, and their fury, so cruel. I will scatter them in Jacob and disperse them in Israel" (Genesis 49:5–7). Anger cost them their blessing, and in Joshua 19, we see that they went to live within the territory of Judah. Simeon's gemstone might have been chrysoprase. Chrysoprase is said to promote joy, self-acceptance, and independence, as well as forgiveness and compassion toward others.

The ancient Babylonians saw Tevet as a time where a gate from the underworld was open, and the ghosts of their ancestors came out to sit in the counsel of the elders during the month, but particularly on the 10th. Like those in heaven who met regularly in a divine council to render judgments for the universe, the divine rulers of the underworld were assisted in their decisions by an elite body called the Anunnaki. Perhaps not so coincidentally, the 10th of Tevet is historically a day of Jewish lamenting and fasting as it was the day of the siege of Jerusalem by the Babylonian king, Nebuchadnezzar.

This is a time for those who do legislative work in the spirit to kick it up a notch. If that's not your thing, don't worry about it, but be extra careful of any deals, contracts, or partnerships entered into this month.

One tradition associates Tevet with the liver, which does make sense as we are processing our anger this month. Potentially, this is a good time to do a liver cleanse. An easy cleanse is to drink warm lemon water first thing in the morning. One can also use Milk Thistle in the herbal form, which is a powerful liver cleanser. Remember how we have it in flower essence form? Anger tends to be stored in the liver, and just as the herbal form cleanses impurities and toxins there, the essence form works with toxic emotions stored in your liver.

Many regard Tevet as a good time for fasting, which can be to whatever degree you feel comfortable with. This can be as simple as eating whole, unprocessed foods for the month. The liver is the purifier of the entire body, so the potential for better overall health is enormous.

As we close out Hanukkah, the word Hanukkah means "dedication." As Hanukkah celebrates the rededication of the temple, we need to remember that our bodies have now become the temple. Jesus said, "The eye is the light of the body, so if your eye is healthy your whole body will be filled with light, but if your eye is evil, your whole body will be filled with darkness" (Matthew 6:22–23). We can also rededicate ourselves to respectful treatment of our body. Self-Heal flower essence will help you intuitively know what to do and motivate you to carry it out.

Tevet טבת

I have yet to understand how time works during the month of Tevet. There appears to be a battle over time. The enemy is looking to change it, and God is seeking to multiply it. Pray for the latter, and ask for eyes to see the enemy's plans to manipulate or change your times. Ask God to override your natural constraints for his purposes.

The constellation is Capricorn the goat. This is a goat with a fishy tail. In ancient Judaism, the goat was a sacrifice or sin offering, and the term "scapegoat" is derived from this. The fish has long been a sign of those who have been redeemed as a result of the sacrifice of the Messiah. Hand all that stuff over to Jesus!

Our gate is the Miphkad Gate, which means assignment, appointment, mandate or numbering. The word Miphkad for a little more context, was used in three places in the Bible; David counting his fighting men, (2 Samuel 24:9; 1 Chronicles 21:5), Hezekiah appointing people into positions (2 Chronicles 31:13) and an appointed area of the temple for sacrifice. (Ezekiel 43:21) It's also called the Inspection Gate, the Gathering Gate, and the Judgment Gate. Here, we need to allow God's good eye to inspect our condition and raise us up to a higher standard, to burn out the dross so we can receive a new assignment.

Month at a Glance
Shevat שבט

Starts in January or February

Meaning: Unknown

Blessing: Imperceptible shifts for new fruit

Area of Healing: Letting go of unproductive areas you base your identity

Action Needed: Seek wisdom and righteousness in your endeavors, start new things

Warfare: Fight fear of change, complacency, the comfort zone

Holidays: New Year for trees

Tribe: Rueben

Gem: Carnelian

Gate: Ephraim Gate

Constellation: Aquarius the water bearer

Decans: Southern fish, Pegasus the winged horse, Cygnus the swan

Shevat שבט

Shevat שבט

We're jumping the gun and celebrating spring in the dead of winter this month. Shevat is the month of silent new beginnings and the New Year for trees. Judaism has several new years in it. It's like our calendar year, the school year, and the fiscal year for some businesses. The 15th of Shevat is the beginning of the new year for the purposes of tithing fruit. It's now become a type of Arbor Day for Israel, and if you'd like to participate, some organizations will plant an olive tree there for you. Supposedly, on this day, there is a seasonal shift, one that we can't even detect, where the tree focuses on the coming year's fruit.

Numerous verses compare men to trees and our fruits to the deeds and expressions that come out of us. So, too, might we put old seasons behind us and focus forward on the new. In Israel during Shevat, the almond trees begin to blossom. Because they are the first bloomers and the almond looks like an eye, they are said to be "watcher" trees. They keep watch for the spring. Apricots are closely related to the almond. I have one, and it is the first fruit tree to bloom, dangerously early, although not in Shevat in Idaho! It is like they seize the first opportunity. They might be watchers, but I watch them.

The Apricot flower essence gives a person empowerment, strength, and courage during seasonal transitions. It's for keeping your balance when you anticipate that everything is about to change. Shevat is that shift month, the stepping stone to the next place in our lives. The new day will not be welcomed by all because they have become too acquainted and familiar with the types and shadows of yesterday.

Late winter is also when we prune fruit trees so that they become more fruitful. If some things are taken from you, it might possibly be for the greater good. You might also look at what things in your life are unproductive, no longer needed, or taking you in a direction you don't want to go. Purple Archangel flower essence can help you sort through some of that.

When I was praying about what to include here, I had a vision of domino tiles set up in a line falling and a sense that we needed to be careful what we set in motion. This is a good time to start new things; that little push can make a big impact, but it will also be hard to mitigate the damage if we set off the

Shevat שבט

wrong things. Wisdom is a big deal this month, as I'll explain later. Solomon talks about wisdom here in Proverbs 3:18. "She is a tree of life to those who take hold of her, and those who hold her fast will be blessed."

The alphabet letter associated with Shevat is *tzadi*, which means righteous one. A *tzaddik* uses his ordinary activities for a higher purpose and looks for the spiritual implications of the mundane. Everything does double duty. When he eats, it's not just for enjoyment; he considers how to eat to better serve God. This can mean that we eat for health and nourishment, to have energy to do what we need to, but also to watch which tree we are feeding from, and to stay with the tree of life. (Excuse me while I shut down news media.)

Our constellation is Aquarius. This shows a man pouring water from a vessel into the mouth of the Southern Fish. Water is symbolized consistently in Scripture as Spirit, and in many ways throughout Judaism, it is a metaphor for the Torah. Fish represent God's people, an outpouring of the Spirit, and knowledge for those positioned to receive. I vaguely remember running around in a dream during Shevat yelling, "I am a fish with my mouth wide open!" That's probably as good a declaration for the month as any.

In Mark 14, Jesus tells his disciples to go into the city where "a man carrying a large jug of water will meet you." This was in preparation for the Last Supper, when Jesus wrapped up some matters with

Shevat שבט

the disciples and spent quality time with them before everything changed.

When we look at the story of the gospel in the constellations in context with the other months, this is the time when Christ ascended so that we could have the Holy Spirit.

One of the qualities of water is that it always flows to the lowest spot. The outpouring of wisdom that comes from God flows to the most humble vessel. Moses "the most humble of men" if he does say so himself in Numbers 12:3) began teaching the Torah on the first of Shevat. He saw himself as a mere vessel in the hands of the Lord. His purpose was solely to draw wisdom from the Source and to pour out the water of God's Word to his people. He died five weeks later.

That brings me back to purpose and the tzaddik. I have been reading about the exact process of becoming a tzaddik or righteous one, which involves flawed people who excelled at their intended purpose. But you need to wade through a whole lot of fulfilling the law while holding up the failures at doing so to the light first. The tzaddiks were committed in an area that meant something to them and did not tolerate mediocrity or compromise. They may have messed up in the other areas of their lives, but those things were not what they were known for, by God or by others. "A tzaddik will flourish like a date palm. He will grow like a cedar in Lebanon. Planted in the house of the LORD, They will flourish in the courts of our God. They will still

Shevat שבט

yield fruit in old age; They shall be full of sap and very green" (Psalm 92:12).

What is that thing for you? That place where you care so much and have a natural inclination toward excellence? Do that. Seek righteousness and wisdom in that area.

That doesn't mean we blow off other areas in terms of righteousness, however. That brings me to Reuben, the tribe that correlates with Shevat. Reuben, "turbulent as the waters," said Jacob, was "the first sign of my strength, excelling in honor, excelling in power" (Genesis 49:3–4). Except when he wasn't. The time that he wasn't cost him his rights as firstborn. He wasn't disowned or disinherited, but he was demoted. His stone might have been carnelian. Freedom Flowers has a Carnelian essence. Our take on Carnelian is that it anchors you in the here and now, stimulating creativity, motivation, concentration, and endurance.

The gate of the month is the Ephraim Gate. Ephraim means "double fruit," which is a great sentiment over our new year of trees. The double-portion is given to the firstborn (what Reuben should have had) and is our promise as we go through training and refining to see our callings fulfilled.

Other appropriate essences this month are Sunflower for the humility and Sage for incorporating wisdom. Trumpet Vine allows you to let that living water flow to others instead of keeping it contained. With Wormwood, you can release the old, and with Apricot, you can move into the new.

Month at a Glance
Adar אדר

Starts in February or March

Meaning: Strength

Blessing: Joy

Area of Healing: Identity

Action Needed: Look for hidden resources, see God working in your circumstances

Warfare: Enemy reaps what he sows, use laughter as a weapon

Holidays: Purim

Tribe: Issachar

Gem: Lapis

Gate: Prison Gate

Constellation: Pisces the fish

Decans: The Band, Cepheus the crowned king, Andromeda the chained woman

Adar אדר

Adar אדר

Welcome to Adar! We are down to the last month of the year, and we are going out joyfully and walking in our identity. "When Adar begins, joy enters," as the common Jewish saying goes. As we are ending the year, we are also looking at ending certain seasons in our lives. Last month, we gained a sense of the new. Let's be deliberate about what we are intentionally leaving behind. If you've been following along all year, we've set some strong intentions about what we were walking out of last Nisan, so it's time to look back on how far we've come.

We also celebrate the hidden or masked miracles. Adar means "strength" and the associated letter is the *kuf*, which symbolizes the masquerade. A parallel was drawn in the story of Purim in the book of Esther when a miracle happened and God was not even mentioned. (The root of Esther in Hebrew is *hester,* meaning "hidden.") God was entirely central to the story, yet his presence was not clearly written into it. The events he orchestrated were covered with many layers of seeming coincidences, political schemings, and natural causes and effects. It's up to us to see and attribute it to God or to write it all off as luck. Throughout the Bible, we have story after story of dramatic rescues: seas parting, mountain tops on fire, plagues descending on enemies, and so much more. All these clearly show the hand of God. But other moments might seem all too common, when God is saying, "I am here now, just as I always have been and always will be here for you. Not just when the sea splits or when my presence overwhelms you, but when you choose to see me."

Adar's holiday, Purim, celebrates the story of Esther, yet there is a big difference between wearing a mask and being hidden. Think of the Mardi Gras masks that come out during the same season as Adar. They are brilliant attention-getting devices that reveal the fact that you are hiding who you really are. Your masks are a barrier to intimacy with people and with God.

For a time, Esther needed to conceal her identity; however, she also could not have fulfilled her destiny without revealing who she really was. As in our tribe of the month (Issachar), timing is everything.

This is a time to see and show your true identity. Freedom and joy are contingent on you being you.

You can only hide behind a conditioning of showing others what you believe is acceptable for so long. Come out, come out! Skullcap, Goldenrod, and Boxwood are essences that help with that.

Is it leap year? If so, then Adar is repeated. Adar 1 is known as a pregnant month. Purim is celebrated in Adar 2 to properly connect with Passover.

Adar is considered the month of good fortune. The constellation is Pisces the fish. There are two of them, which matters. This is the month that Peter had to get the coin from the fish's mouth to pay taxes. Be asking about where you personally need to look for your provision. Throughout the New Testament, fish were a symbol of provision. Star Thistle flower essence helps to reverse worry over finances.

Consider that Pisces consists of two fish, swimming in different directions. In Aquarius with Shevat, a fish was in that constellation, too, receiving the water being poured out. As the one fish (also symbolic of God's people) swims up, so we move toward relationship with our heavenly Father. And as the other fish swims outward, we move toward relationship with the world around us. The degree to which we are successful in either is in our ability to be true to our design. Both are held back by a band that binds them to Cetus the sea monster, but Aries, a symbol of Jesus, also has his paw on the band in between, intervening.

Purim, established by Mordecai and Esther, is a symbol of what was meant for evil being turned for good. Haman was hung on the tree he meant where he meant to hang Mordecai. Haman threw lots, and they landed on the 13th of Adar to kill Jews. He thought he picked a good time since the 7th of Adar was the day Moses died. Haman thought this meant that he would undo everything that Moses had done. What he didn't realize was that Moses's birthday was also the 7th of Adar, so the date turned out to be a day of rebirth. So many things in this story were hidden and later revealed.

It's truly a month to celebrate God overturning your circumstances in your favor. Whatever was meant for your destruction is coming back at your adversary. Laughter is the weapon of warfare for the month and holds the key to our breakthrough. We can laugh at our fears, our worries, and our adversities. Zinnia and Thimbleberry flower essences can help with that.

The gate of the month is the Prison Gate. The gatekeepers named here were Shallum, Akkub, Talmon, and Ahiman. These four were brothers, by the way. (See 1 Chronicles 9:17–18.) Shallum means retribution. Akkub means insidious; Talmon means oppressive.

I don't know about you, but I can see the plot of Haman in those names. Then we get to Ahiman, which means "my brother is a gift." Say what, now? Those guys? The thing was, the very evil that was about to annihilate the Jewish people is what brought Esther out of hiding her true identity and made it possible to thoroughly eradicate their enemies. I invite you to read Esther this month and look at it in context of this gate and turning the tables on the enemy through the revealing of your identity.

Our self-expression is on display this month, and the flower essence Calendula can help you weigh your words and communicate with warmth and sensitivity. I had a dream during Adar about washing my hair (mindsets, renewal) with calendula shampoo.

The tribe of the month is Issachar, famous for their innate ability to understand the times and seasons so that people could know what to do when. (This is the whole idea behind this book series.) The tribe was also closely connected with Zebulon, and both were supposed to be bringing out the hidden things and the treasures from the sand and sea. The stone for Issachar is a dark blue stone, probably the lapis. Lapis is said to be a protective stone that blocks the bad intentions of others and their desire to wish harm on a person. It returns the negative energy to its source. On an energetic level, it's similar to Haman receiving back what he was putting out. Lapis also encourages self-awareness and self-expression and reveals inner truth. No more masks!

Adar אדר

Your Birth Month

Now that you see the difference in the Hebrew calendar and the Mazzaroth vs. the secular timelines and astrology, a natural question is, "Does my birth month mean anything for me personally?" Or "I'm an Aries; what does that say within God's system?"

I like these questions because they're not fear-based, but I won't answer them for you. I will, however, help you explore this topic.

Dr. Christopher Motley is a Christian chiropractor who believes that it does make a difference what time of year you were born. He says embryonic development is affected by celestial and lunar phases, and the gravitational forces on different mineral, ion, and blood composition affect our chemical balance and biochemistry, which correlate to our personalities. Nutrients are transported by the fluids in our bodies (amniotic fluid) similar to the way tides are affected by the moon. This has no real bearing on destiny per astrology but could explain people why born under certain star signs have similar traits.

On one hand, a star announced Jesus's birth. God showed Abraham that he would be the father of many nations by using the stars. Abraham begat Isaac, who begat Jacob, who fathered the twelve tribes that represent the twelve constellations.

On the other hand, Jeremiah 10:2 says, "Do not be terrified by the signs of the heavens although the nations are terrified by them." Some rabbis interpret that to mean that although the stars have influence, God's people are not subject to these influences. Psalm 19 also tells us that the stars declare the glory of God, and Genesis 1:14 says they are for "signs, seasons, days and years." Signs is the word *'outh* meaning, "a signal, flag, beacon, monument, omen, evidence, mark, miracle, sign, token." In other words, there is no indication that they determine your identity.

Ian Clayton, in his teaching titled, "Mazzaroth," says that the voice of the stars has been corrupted. He has another teaching, "Untethered," that walks you through some renunciations and into the court of heaven where you bring the twelve constellations for judgment for what they have been speaking into your life. This is definitely worth doing if you have been involved in astrology in the past, and in any case, you can always benefit from prayer and decrees that only what's of God gets through to you.

I have had some experience with stepping out from under the influence of the celestial systems. I had never really given much attention to Mercury in retrograde. "Other" people always had this problem, and it was a convenient scapegoat for all their glitches and communication issues. When Freedom Flowers started growing and I had to bring on staff, Mercury in retrograde hit us broadside. Customers were repeatedly sent wrong packages, stuff went missing, and we dealt with many misunderstandings and problems with the website, email, and printer. I thought, *Gee, this sounds just like Mercury in retrograde*. I googled, and sure enough, we were in it. Now, as united staff within Freedom Flowers, we make a point of declaring that we are not participating in the upcoming Mercury in retrograde, but we are here to help the people who are. We have had no problems since then.

We also see an uptick in customers reaching out a few days to a week prior to the new moon. Experienced flower essence users suddenly forget basic information, such as how to use them, or they need reassurance or permission in their choices. Others just need a lot of hand holding in various ways. My hypothesis about this is that we subconsciously know a shift is coming, and most people are not comfortable with change. We haven't felt the need to do new moon renunciations or declare ourselves free of these effects, because we as staff aren't noticing any new moon effects. We just deal with the secondary issues of being frazzled and our patience being tested from working with so many people who suddenly seem to be regressing.

We mark the calendar and know that we need to be taking care of ourselves during those days, allowing more time for everybody, and the struggles will pass in a couple days. Buy us a shot of whiskey if you see us during the last week of a lunar month.

So what about just taking the good parts of astrology and leaving the bad? Well, I think we still need to be careful where our information comes from. We did a little experiment in the Healing in the Hebrew Months Facebook group and looked at the Hebraic data for our birth month to see if it felt accurate. Everybody who reported back could see themes present in that month that ran throughout their life. I, for one, saw my life's focus and core values in mine.

To do this, we first ran our date of birth through a Hebrew date calculator, making sure to check the "after sundown" box if we were born in the evening. Some of us found out we were born on Jewish holidays. Some of us found out we were born on a month associated with a different constellation than our secular astrological sign. That gives us our Hebraic birth month, and you can look over the information in this book while thinking in terms of your life rather than just a month in a cycle.

Remember the three decans that go with each constellation that rise approximately every ten days within that month. You can divide the month into thirds, list the decans in order, and see which third your birthday falls into for a rough idea of how these might relate to you.

In the same manner, you can look at the sons of the patriarch of the tribe that corresponds to your month and divide the month by the number of sons. List them in birth order and research the "son in your sign."

For example, Nisan means "to move or to start." That would be me. I procrastinate, but it is never when I start something. I move into action as soon as possible on a matter. Nisan is also known as the month of redemption. I have thought that my life's work is actually about redemption. I know I do a lot of things, but the chord running through all of it is redeeming what no one will touch so that it's useful to God's people. I also have a larger picture of the blood than most people have and know that more revelation will come to me in that area.

The tribe that corresponds to this month is Gad, which means "good fortune." I am good with money, and I have enough that I have many options, although that can be taken many ways. Gad's prophecy was that a troop shall overcome him, but he will triumph at last (Genesis 49:19). Yup, that relates. Moses addresses executing the justice of the Lord. I just received a prophetic word about that prior to doing this exercise. Confirmation already! Then I looked at Gad's sons and divided them across the month. The one corresponding to me was Ziphion: visionary, seeing what others cannot, and entrepreneurial-minded. Uh-huh. There's a struggle with the incongruence of vision vs. walking into reality. Sigh.

The liberation from Egypt happened during Nisan. The decan that was up at that time was Cassopeia, and Frances Rolleston says the principle star means "the freed." "Whom the son (Aries/lamb) sets free is free indeed." Oh, and I tend to learn really significant lessons or receive large measures of freedom at Passover.

Your turn if you so choose. I haven't tracked with the connection between Hebraic birthdates and giftings and callings for long. There might be better ways to research this. I would use the same disclaimer they do in the newspaper section, "for entertainment purposes only." I would also look at this as confirmation of your true design rather than new direction or insight. Be careful what you allow to define you.

Onward

If you're here, either you've made it through one revolution, or you've just read the book. Either way, you're clearly interested enough to go to the next level. This is one book in a series of three.

Healing in the Hebrew Months

Coming Fall 2019

The first book in the series, *Healing in the Hebrew Months*, is by Leah Lesesne. She is an inner-healing practitioner and is the founder of Captive Thought Therapy, a type of tapping exercise similar to EFT (Emotional Freedom Technique). I had looked into

EFT in the past but was never really comfortable with the verbal statements one has to make. They use a one-size-fits-all tapping pattern, which is easy to learn but is not as effective for some issues. She also teaches you how to incorporate a little bit of bilateral stimulation that is used in EMDR therapy.

Her book is structured similarly to this with a monthly plan for healing. If you're a *show me chapter and verse* type of person (or you know one you want to introduce to these books), she unpacks the biblical references to each month and what was going on with Israel during those times. From there she identifies emotional themes in each month and gives you a practical activation to engage with healing throughout the month. Learning one tapping exercise per month is not all that difficult.

Del Hungerford, PhD is the third author in our series. She creates music using healing frequencies that enhances cognitive function, heals the emotions, awakens intuition, and engages our senses. Her research into musical frequencies is highly respected by many in the music community.

Her book focuses on the connection between Hebrew letters, their gematria, musical frequencies, the A=432 concert pitch, and the blessings found within each letter. The letters demonstrate the overall character of God and are meant to assist in our daily walk of intimacy with YHVH. As we learn to walk in that intimate place with him, musicians and non-musicians alike receive healing.

Del had an encounter where Jesus showed her "beyond the veil" in the tabernacle. During that experience, she watched the priest sing the names of God. As he did so, frequencies, in the form of colored ribbons, floated around the holy of holies. Each sung musical note intermixed with a name of God and danced about the room, interacting with the stones on the priest's breastplate, along with all the items in and on the ark of the covenant.

You can apply the information in any of these books by itself, or you can layer them together for a more complete picture and healing process. A cord of three-strands is not quickly broken (Ecclesiastes 4:12).

Del also has a Song of the Month club that includes a new song composed with the frequencies of the Hebrew letters and an activation to help you heal as well as practice seeing in the spirit and relating with God.

I, of course, have my Times and Seasons subscription box that includes a flower essence blend to augment the healing in the month, a piece of gemstone jewelry, and a letter about the coming month. If you'd like only the essences to use with this book, I have the monthly combinations available on my site in the store under "package deals."

Onward

References

[1] Jewish Calendar: Judaism 101
http://www.jewfaq.org/calendar.htm Accessed 7/11/19
[2] Jewish Calendar: Judaism 101
http://www.jewfaq.org/calendar.htm Accessed 7/11/19
[3] The Jewish Leap Year Time and Date.com
https://www.timeanddate.com/date/jewish-leap-year.html Accessed 7/11/19
[4] Leap Year Calculator Torah Calc
https://www.torahcalc.com/leapyears/ 6/25/19
[5] Wescott, W.W. (trans) Sefer Yetzirah: The Book of Formation and the Thirty-two Paths of Wisdom 1893
http://www.iapsop.com/ssoc/1893__westcott__sepher_yetzirah.pdf Accessed 7/13/19
[6] Wisnefsky, Rabbi Moshe "Jewish Astrology?" Ask Moses http://www.askmoses.com/en/article/424,60378/Jewish-Astrology.html#articlepage Accessed 7/13/19
[7] Abarim Publications http://www.abarim-publications.com/Meaning/Gad.html Accessed 6/21/19
[8] Abarim Publications http://www.abarim-publications.com/Meaning/Asher.html 6/21/19
[9] Abarim Publications http://www.abarim-publications.com/Meaning/Benjamin.html 6/21/19
[10] Abarim Publications http://www.abarim-publications.com/Meaning/Zebulun.html 6/21/19
[11] Abarim Publications http://www.abarim-publications.com/Meaning/Judah.html 6/21/19
[12] Abarim Publications http://www.abarim-publications.com/Meaning/Naphtali.html 6/21/19
[13] Abarim Publications http://www.abarim-publications.com/Meaning/Levi.html 6/21/19
[14] Abarim Publications http://www.abarim-publications.com/Meaning/Dan.html 6/21/19
[15] Abarim Publications http://www.abarim-publications.com/Meaning/Joseph.html 6/21/19
[16] Abarim Publications http://www.abarim-publications.com/Meaning/Simeon.html 6/21/19
[17] Abarim Publications http://www.abarim-publications.com/Meaning/Reuben.html 6/21/19

References

[18] Abarim Publications http://www.abarim-publications.com/Meaning/Issachar.html 6/21/19
[19] Rolleston, Frances "The Mazzaroth" 1862
[20] "Heliacal Rising" The Ascension Glossary https://ascensionglossary.com/index.php/Heliacal_rising Accessed 7/13/19
[21] Callimachus, Hymns and Epigrams. Lycophron. Aratus. Translated by Mair, A. W. & G. R. Loeb Classical Library Volume 129. London: William Heinemann, 1921.
[22] Rolleston, Frances "The Mazzaroth" 1862
[23] Charles, R.H. (trans) Book of Enoch 1917 http://www.sacred-texts.com/bib/boe/boe075.htm Accessed 7/13/19
[24] Josephus, Flavius "Antiquities of the Jews Book 1"
[25] Hertzenberg, Stephanie "What is the Oldest Book in the Bible?" Beliefnet https://www.beliefnet.com/faiths/christianity/what-is-the-oldest-book-in-the-bible.aspx 6/20/19
[26] Rolleston, Frances "The Mazzaroth" 1862
[27] Rolleston, Frances "The Mazzaroth" 1862
[28] Allen, Richard H "Star Names: Their Lore and Meaning" Dover Publications 1963
[29] "Diyn" Old Testament Lexicon https://www.biblestudytools.com/lexicons/hebrew/nas/diyn.html Accessed 7/11/19
[30] Cratylus, Plato
[31] Strong, James. 1890. Strong's Exhaustive Concordance of the Bible. Abingdon Press H5306
[32] Strong, James. 1890. Strong's Exhaustive Concordance of the Bible. Abingdon Press H124
[33] Strong, James. 1890. Strong's Exhaustive Concordance of the Bible. Abingdon Press H306
[34] "Zabargad Island" Wikipedia https://en.wikipedia.org/wiki/Zabargad_Island
[35] Nickalls, Netanel "The Stones to Build on the Foundation of Yeshua" https://soundcloud.com/netanel_777/sets/the-stones-to-build-on-the?fbclid=IwAR2ScfNNyINQdG1N0TtESasF7pqbCXuNyOvJe6MpqV6lHnEIVazdyNdTf8U
[36] Josephus, Flavius "Antiquities of the Jews Book 1"

References

37 The Midrash: Numbers Rabba Sacred Texts https://www.sacred-texts.com/jud/mhl/mhl08.htm Accessed 7/13/19
38 Mishneh Torah, Hil. Klei Hamikdash 10:11
39 King, Hobart M Flourescent Minerals" geology.com https://geology.com/articles/fluorescent-minerals/ Accessed 7/12/19
40 "Rosh Chodesh 101" My Jewish Learning https://www.myjewishlearning.com/article/rosh-chodesh-101/
41 Midrashic work Pirkei de-Rabbi Eliezer
42 "Awakening From Above: The Month of Nissan and Passover" Iyyun Center for Jewish Spirituality http://iyyun.com/hebrew-calendar/awakening-from-above-the-month-of-nissan-and-passover Accessed 7/13/19
43 The Babylonian Talmud (Tractate Rosh HaShana 11a)
44 Abarim Publications http://www.abarim-publications.com/Meaning/Gad.html Accessed 7/13/19
45 Abarim Publications http://www.abarim-publications.com/Meaning/Gad.html 6/21/19
46 The Midrash: Numbers Rabba Sacred Texts https://www.sacred-texts.com/jud/mhl/mhl08.htm Accessed 7/13/19
47 Aries Constellation Constellation Guide https://www.constellation-guide.com/constellation-list/aries-constellation/ 6/25/19
48 Strong, James. 1890. Strong's Exhaustive Concordance of the Bible. Abingdon Press H475
49 Abarim Publications http://www.abarim-publications.com/Meaning/Zaccur.html 6/11/19
50 The Name Meaning https://www.thenamemeaning.com/imri/ 6/11/19
51 Strong, James. 1890. Strong's Exhaustive Concordance of the Bible. Abingdon Press H5570
52 Bible Hub https://biblehub.com/topical/m/meremoth.htm 6/1/19
53 Bible Study Tools https://www.biblestudytools.com/dictionary/urijah/ 6/11/19
54 Bible Study Tools https://www.biblestudytools.com/dictionary/koz/ 6/11/19

References

55 Abarim Publications http://www.abarim-publications.com/Meaning/Meshullam.html 6/11/19

56 Abarim Publications http://www.abarim-publications.com/Meaning/Berechiah.html Accessed 7/26/19

57 Strong, James. 1890. Strong's Exhaustive Concordance of the Bible. Abingdon Press H4898

58 Abarim Publications http://www.abarim-publications.com/Meaning/Zadok.html 6/11/19

59 Abarim Publications http://www.abarim-publications.com/Meaning/Baana.htm 6/11/19

60 Hesiod, "Works and Days" https://www.ellopos.net/elpenor/greek-texts/ancient-greece/hesiod/works-days.asp Accessed 7/15/19

61 Orion Constellation, Constellation Guide https://www.constellation-guide.com/constellation-list/orion-constellation/ 6/25/19

62 Orion Constellation, Constellation Guide https://www.constellation-guide.com/constellation-list/orion-constellation/ 6/25/19

63 Philogos "A Constellation of Theories Regarding the Nebulous History of Orion" Forward https://forward.com/culture/181082/a-constellation-of-theories-regarding-the-nebulous/

64 Philogos "A Constellation of Theories Regarding the Nebulous History of Orion" Forward https://forward.com/culture/181082/a-constellation-of-theories-regarding-the-nebulous/

65 Hirsch, Emil; Seligsohn, M; Bacher, Wilhelm "Nimrod" http://www.jewishencyclopedia.com/articles/11548-nimrod Accessed 7/15/19

66 "Eridanus" Constellation Guide https://www.constellation-guide.com/constellation-list/eridanus-constellation/ Accessed 7/15/19

67 "Auriga Constellation" Constellation Guide https://www.constellation-guide.com/constellation-list/auriga-constellation/ 6/25/19

68 Jastow, Morris Jr, McCurdy, Frederic J "Asher, Tribe and Territory" Jewish Encyclopedia 1906

69 Midrash Numbers Rabba

70 "Peridot Healing Properties" Charms of Light https://www.charmsoflight.com/peridot-healing-properties

References

[71] Rhoads, Betty "Asher = Baltics" https://the-red-thread.net/Asher-by-Betmatrho.html

[72] "Playing Praise on a Bitter Tamborine: The Story of Miriam" Daughter's Dialogue https://daughtersdialogue.wordpress.com/2013/08/18/playing-praise-on-a-bitter-tambourine-the-story-of-miriam/

[73] "Shav'ot" Judaism 101 http://www.jewfaq.org/holidayc.htm Accessed 7/15/19

[74] McClure, Bruce "Gemini? Here's Your Constellation" EarthSky https://earthsky.org/astronomy-essentials/gemini-heres-your-constellation 2/17/17

[75] Abarim Publications http://www.abarim-publications.com/Meaning/Jehoiada.html 6/11/19

[76] Strong, James. 1890. Strong's Exhaustive Concordance of the Bible. Abingdon Press H6454

[77] Abarim Publications http://www.abarim-publications.com/Meaning/Meshullam.html 6/11/19

[78] Strong, James. 1890. Strong's Exhaustive Concordance of the Bible. Abingdon Press H1152

[79] "Jasper" https://www.crystalvaults.com/crystal-encyclopedia/jasper Accessed 7/15/19

[80] Babylonian Talmud: Tractate Shabbath Folio 89

[81] Strong, James. 1890. Strong's Exhaustive Concordance of the Bible. Abingdon Press H2586

[82] Strong, James. 1890. Strong's Exhaustive Concordance of the Bible. Abingdon Press H2182

[83] King, Hobart M "Quartz" geology.com https://geology.com/minerals/quartz.shtml

[84] Hall, Judy "The Crystal Bible" Walking Stick Press 2003

[85] Zimmerman, Kim A "Cancer Constellation: Facts About the Crab" https://www.space.com/16970-cancer-constellation.html 7/15/17

[86] "Cancer Constellation" Constellation Guide https://www.constellation-guide.com/constellation-list/cancer-constellation/ 6/25/19

[87] Rolleston, Frances "The Mazzaroth" 1862

[88] "Properties of the Number 20" Riding the Beast https://www.ridingthebeast.com/numbers/nu20.php Accessed 7/15/19

References

[89] "Leo Constellation" Constellation Guide https://www.constellation-guide.com/constellation-list/leo-constellation/ 6/25/19

[90] Hall, Judy "The Crystal Bible" Walking Stick Press 2003

[91] "Blue Chalcedony Meanings and Uses " Crystal Vaults https://www.crystalvaults.com/crystal-encyclopedia/blue-chalcedony 6/27/19

[92] Bible Hub https://biblehub.com/topical/m/malchiah.htmI 6/11/19

[93] Strong, James. 1890. Strong's Exhaustive Concordance of the Bible. Abingdon Press H5321

[94] Strong, James. 1890. Strong's Exhaustive Concordance of the Bible. Abingdon Press H5869

[95] Platt, Rutherford H "The Forgotten Books of Eden" Testament of Naphtali 1:18 1926

[96] Abarim Publications http://www.abarim-publications.com/Meaning/Shallun.html 6/11/19

[97] Abarim Publications http://www.abarim-publications.com/Meaning/Col-hozeh.html 6/11/19

[98] Abarim Publications http://www.abarim-publications.com/Meaning/Mizpah.html 6/11/19

[99] Amethyst definition, Merriam Webster's Student Dictionary http://wordcentral.com/cgi-bin/student?amethyst

[100] Judaism 101: Rosh Hashanah. http://www.jewfaq.org/holiday2.htm

[101] "Lupus Constellation" Constellation Guide https://www.constellation-guide.com/constellation-list/lupus-constellation/ 6/25/19

[102] Hall, Judy "The Crystal Bible" Walking Stick Press 2003

[103] Abarim Publications http://www.abarim-publications.com/Meaning/Tekoa.html 6/11/19

[104] "Turquoise Meanings and Uses" Crystal Vaults https://www.crystalvaults.com/crystal-encyclopedia/turquoise 6/28/19

[105] "Turquoise Meanings and Uses" Crystal Vaults https://www.crystalvaults.com/crystal-encyclopedia/turquoise 6/28/19

[106] Hall, Judy "The Crystal Bible" Walking Stick Press 2003

[107] Charles, R.H. (trans) The Book of Jubilees or The little Genesis. London, A. and C. 1902

References

[108] Ogbonnaya, Adonijah "Awakening the God Impulse" https://youtu.be/3ZRdu621HhI Accessed 7/13/19

[109] Ogbonnaya, Adonijah "Awakening the God Impulse" https://youtu.be/3ZRdu621HhI Accessed 7/13/19

[110] "Draco Constellation" Constellation Guide https://www.constellation-guide.com/constellation-list/draco-constellation/ Accessed 7/13/19

[111] Hall, Judy "The Crystal Bible" Walking Stick Press 2003

[112] Oakes, Liz "Chrysoprase aka Green Chalcedony" https://www.healing-crystals-for-you.com/chrysoprase.html 6/28/19

[113] Ancient Mesopotamian Beliefs in the Afterlife - Ancient …. https://www.ancient.eu/article/701/ancient-mesopotamian-beliefs-in-the-afterlife/

[114] Strong, James. 1890. Strong's Exhaustive Concordance of the Bible. Abingdon Press H4662

[115] "Nine Things Every Jew Should Know About the Month of Adar" Chabad https://www.chabad.org/holidays/purim/article_cdo/aid/2863908/jewish/9-Things-Every-Jew-Should-Know-About-the-Month-of-Adar.htm Accessed 7/13/19

[116] "The Month of Adar According to Sefer Yetzirah" Gal Einai https://www.inner.org/times/adar/adar.htm Accessed 7/13/19

[117] "Esther: Hidden Beauty". www.chabad.org. Accessed 7/13/19

[118] Abarim Publications http://www.abarim-publications.com/Meaning/Shallum.html 6/11/19)

[119] Strong, James. 1890. Strong's Exhaustive Concordance of the Bible. Abingdon Press H6126

[120] Strong, James. 1890. Strong's Exhaustive Concordance of the Bible. Abingdon Press H2929

[121] Strong, James. 1890. Strong's Exhaustive Concordance of the Bible. Abingdon Press H289

[122] Hall, Judy "The Crystal Bible" Walking Stick Press 2003

[123] "Lapis Lazuli Healing Properties" Charms of Light https://www.charmsoflight.com/lapis-lazuli-healing-properties 6/28/19

[124] Motley, Christopher. "Development and the Stars" Facebook 4/17/19

References

https://www.facebook.com/doctormotley/posts/2588455854558142

[125] Strong, James. 1890. Strong's Exhaustive Concordance of the Bible. Abingdon Press H226

[126] Awakening From Above: The Month of Nissan and Passover" Iyyun Center for Jewish Spirituality http://iyyun.com/hebrew-calendar/awakening-from-above-the-month-of-nissan-and-passover Accessed 7/13/19

[127] Abarim Publications http://www.abarim-publications.com/Meaning/Gad.html Accessed 7/11/19

About the Author

Seneca Schurbon

Seneca started making and selling flower essences at the ripe old age of five. Her company Freedom Flowers, based in the Idaho wilderness, is the perfect marriage of the natural and spiritual for emotional healing. She actively works to take back the things of God that have been ceded over to the enemy, by looking for Gods original purpose for his creation. Seneca also enjoys research rabbit trails, exploring ideas, and dragging others along for the ride.

FB: www.facebook.com/freedomfloweressence

Instagram: @FreedomFlowerEssence

Website: www.Freedom-Flowers.com

Other Books by the Author

Flower Power: Essences that Heal

is a practical guide that reveals the power of flower essences to heal emotional imbalances in humans (and their pets!).

Flower essences can help you move past fears and self-limiting beliefs, work through trauma, propel you to achieve your goals, improve your relationships, diffuse stress, anxiety, and anger; contribute to healthy spiritual development, and much, much more!

With compelling, intuitive information on more than 100 flower essences and sections addressing trauma, physical healing, and fulfilling your destiny, this handy guide will help you embrace and employ the potential of flower frequencies to help restore the balance and symmetry of a robust, vibrant and satisfying life.

Body Coaching: Losing Weight Through Positive Self-talk

"Body, we need to talk..."

What we say to ourselves and about ourselves matters. Body coaching is a 30-day program of positive self-talk. Taking authority in our spirits over our bodies and giving ourselves the pep talks we've desperately needed.

It's not about will powering your way through another diet or exercise program, it's about partnering your body, mind, and spirit together so that you can experience the breakthroughs you've been longing for.

Broken to Whole: Inner Healing for the Fragmented Soul

Why Aren't You Healed?

Do you ever feel like you continually struggle with certain emotions? Maybe you've tried counseling or various ministries, yet no matter what you do, nothing works.

If traditional prayer and deliverance hasn't cut it, you might be dealing with soul fragments. When we experience a traumatizing event, part of our coping strategy is to wall off a little piece of ourselves in order to contain that emotion. We then go on with life. A fragment is that part of you that's been locked away, inaccessible to healing, until now.

This book is a game-changer in how you'll look at inner healing. We aren't going to beat the drum for repentance and forgiveness although those are beneficial and necessary. Instead, we have made every effort to tell you something you don't know so that you can fill in your missing pieces.

Accessing Your Spiritual Inheritance

It's Your Turn to Go Through the Door

Alice didn't fall down a rabbit hole but she did walk through a mystical doorway in a vision to recover blessings her ancestors failed to claim. When Alice came back and shared her experience, Seneca wasted no time going through her own door. Del's approach differed -- she wound up floating along in her bloodstream!

Through the map we give in our stories, others went through their own doors, leading to better relationships with God, increase in finances, favor, and giftings. Although this book touches on generational curses and how to remove them, we focus on claiming the blessings your family line has lost. However, you'll need to be open to having a vision, and we'll walk you through the step-by-step process of learning to see, so that you, too, can restore your lost generational blessings.
Your hidden inheritance awaits!

www.ingramcontent.com/pod-product-compliance
Lightning Source LLC
Chambersburg PA
CBHW071201070526
44584CB00019B/2877